Language and Culture

Language and Culture

Edited by

Patrick Gleeson
Nancy Wakefield

San Francisco State College

Charles E. Merrill Publishing Company
Columbus, Ohio
A Bell and Howell Company

Library of Congress Catalog Number: 68-16495

2 3 4 5 — 72, 71, 70, 69, 68

Printed in the United States of America

Preface

Language is a subject broad enough to go beyond the limits of a single academic discipline. Yet anthropologists, sociologists, communications engineers, philosophers, linguists, literary critics, and more—each in his own way—must deal with particular language problems. In doing so, as essays in this collection reveal, each writer also illuminates the general nature and function of language. The vantage point of a special discipline is a good one to see at whatever distance the outlines of the whole.

One may at first find little unity underlying the variety of viewpoints and conclusions regarding language, even within the limits of a single anthology. But this is not quite the case. During the past months, while putting together the present collection, sorting out the many useful and interesting essays from those that seemed and still seem essential, the editors have found a handful of shared premises underlying the most valuable contributions to language study. However critically they consider them, students may want to keep the simplest of these premises in mind at the beginning of their study of language:

1) the relation between language and culture is a necessary consideration in any fruitful discussion of language, no matter how

practical or limited in scope it may appear; many fallacies and trivial conclusions follow when this complex relation is overlooked;

2) the relation is reciprocal: the form of language influences (and some would have it *determines*) the form of culture; the form of culture influences the form of language and language change;

3) the study of a given language at its limits is extremely valuable, and leads to an understanding of the potentialities and limitations of the culture and cultural elements otherwise difficult to attain.

In fact all the essays in the present collection seem to share and, hopefully, justify the first premise. In different forms the greater number of them are explicitly concerned to define and inform the second: is it primarily the language or the culture which determines the form of the other? To what extent can language and culture be separately analyzed at all? If so, then how? What are the means? The third premise leads students back to their own disciplines, where they may best judge its truth.

Patrick Gleeson

Nancy Wakefield

Table of Contents

1

Origins, Limits, and General Problems

The following essay was first published in 1921 as the opening
chapter of Edward Sapir's LANGUAGE: AN INTRODUCTION TO
THE STUDY OF SPEECH. Sapir's book influenced more than a generation of American linguists and remains today one of the best
introductions to language study.

In "Language Defined" Sapir begins by remarking that despite its
apparent naturalness language is not a natural function. Then what
is language, and how shall we describe it? What are the implications
of our definition? After arriving at a definition of language (paragraph 7) Sapir begins concentrating on the relation between speech
and experience. What is the function of the arbitrary system of symbolism we call language? To what extent is thought possible without
speech? Sapir's answer to this apparently trivial question is surprising and important. His conclusions lead to the remarkable hypotheses
developed by Benjamin Whorf (outlined in "Science and Linguistics"
in the present collection), and suggest that for psychologists, sociologists, anthropologists, and, indeed, anyone interested in human behavior, the study of language is centrally important.

Language Defined

Edward Sapir

Speech is so familiar a feature of daily life that we rarely pause
to define it. It seems as natural to man as walking, and only less so
than breathing. Yet it needs but a moment's reflection to convince us
that this naturalness of speech is but an illusory feeling. The process
of acquiring speech is, in sober fact, an utterly different sort of thing
from the process of learning to walk. In the case of the latter func-

tion, culture, in other words, the traditional body of social usage, is not seriously brought into play. The child is individually equipped, by the complex set of factors that we term biological heredity, to make all the needed muscular and nervous adjustments that result in walking. Indeed, the very conformation of these muscles and of the appropriate parts of the nervous system may be said to be primarily adapted to the movements made in walking and in similar activities. In a very real sense the normal human being is predestined to walk, not because his elders will assist him to learn the art, but because his organism is prepared from birth, or even from the moment of conception, to take on all those expenditures of nervous energy and all those muscular adaptations that result in walking. To put it concisely, walking is an inherent, biological function of man. 2. Not so language. It is of course true that in a certain sense the individual is predestined to talk, but that is due entirely to the circumstance that he is born not merely in nature, but in the lap of a society that is certain, reasonably certain, to lead him to its traditions. Eliminate society and there is every reason to believe that he will learn to walk, if, indeed, he survives at all. But it is just as certain that he will never learn to talk, that is, to communicate ideas according to the traditional system of a particular society. Or, again, remove the new-born individual from the social environment into which he has come and transplant him to an utterly alien one. He will develop the art of walking in his new environment very much as he would have developed it in the old. But his speech will be completely at variance with the speech of his native environment. Walking, then, is a general human activity that varies only within circumscribed limits as we pass from individual to individual. Its variability is involuntary and purposeless. Speech is a human activity that varies without assignable limit as we pass from social group to social group, because it is a purely historical heritage of the group, the product of long-continued social usage. It varies as all creative effort varies—not as consciously, perhaps, but none the less as truly as do the religions, the beliefs, the customs, and the arts of different peoples. Walking is an organic, an instinctive, function (not, of course, itself an instinct); speech is a non-instinctive, acquired, "cultural" function. 3. There is one fact that has frequently tended to prevent the recognition of language as a merely conventional system of sound symbols, that has seduced the popular mind into attributing to it an instinctive basis that it does not really possess. This is the well-known observation that under the stress of emotion, say of a sudden twinge of pain or of unbridled joy, we do involuntarily give utterance to sounds that the hearer interprets as indicative of the emotion itself. But there is all the difference in the world between such involuntary expression of feeling and the normal type of communication of ideas that is speech. The former kind of utterance is indeed instinctive, but it is non-symbolic; in other words, the sound of pain or the sound of joy does not, as such, indicate the emotion, it does not stand aloof, as it were, and announce that such and such an emotion is being felt. What it does is to serve as a more or less automatic overflow of the emotional energy; in a sense, it is part and parcel of the emotion itself. More-over, such instinctive cries hardly constitute communication in any strict sense. They are not addressed to any one, they are merely over-heard, if heard at all, as the bark of a dog, the sound of approaching footsteps, or the rustling of the wind is heard. If they convey certain ideas to the hearer, it is only in the very general sense in which any and every sound or even any phenomenon in our environment may be said to convey an idea to the perceiving mind. If the involuntary cry of pain which is conventionally represented by "Oh!" be looked upon as a true speech symbol equivalent to some such idea as "I am in great pain," it is just as allowable to interpret the appearance of clouds as an equivalent symbol that carries the definite message "It is likely to rain." A definition of language, however, that is so extended as to cover any type of inference becomes utterly meaningless.

4. The mistake must not be made of identifying our conventional in-terjections (our oh! and ah! and sh!) with the instinctive cries them-selves. These interjections are merely conventional fixations of the natural sounds. They therefore differ widely in various languages in accordance with the specific phonetic genius of each of these. As such they may be considered an integral portion of speech, in the properly cultural sense of the term, being no more identical with the instinctive cries themselves than such words as "cuckoo" and "killdeer" are identi-cal with the cries of the birds they denote or than Rossini's treatment of a storm in the overture to "William Tell" is in fact a storm. In other words, the interjections and sound-imitative words of normal speech are related to their natural prototypes as is art, a purely social or cul-tural thing, to nature. It may be objected that, though the interjections differ somewhat as we pass from language to language, they do never-

theless offer striking family resemblances and may therefore be looked upon as having grown up out of a common instinctive base. But their case is nowise different from that, say, of the varying national modes of pictorial representation. A Japanese picture of a hill both differs from and resembles a typical modern European painting of the same kind of hill. Both are suggested by and both "imitate" the same natural feature. Neither the one nor the other is the same thing as, or, in any intelligible sense, a direct outgrowth of, this natural feature. The two modes of representation are not identical because they proceed from differing historical traditions, are executed with differing pictorial techniques. The interjections of Japanese and English are, just so, suggested by a common natural prototype, the instinctive cries, and are thus unavoidably suggestive of each other. They differ, now greatly, now but little, because they are builded out of historically diverse materials or techniques, the respective linguistic traditions, phonetic systems, speech habits of the two peoples. Yet the instinctive cries as such are practically identical for all humanity, just as the human skeleton or nervous system is to all intents and purposes a "fixed," that is, an only slightly and "accidentally" variable, feature of man's organism.
5. Interjections are among the least important of speech elements. Their discussion is valuable mainly because it can be shown that even they, avowedly the nearest of all language sounds to instinctive utterance, are only superficially of an instinctive nature. Were it therefore possible to demonstrate that the whole of language is traceable, in its ultimate historical and psychological foundations, to the interjections, it would still not follow that language is an instinctive activity. But, as a matter of fact, all attempts so to explain the origin of speech have been fruitless. There is no tangible evidence, historical or otherwise, tending to show that the mass of speech elements and speech processes has evolved out of the interjections. These are a very small and functionally insignificant proportion of the vocabulary of language; at no time and in no linguistic province that we have record of do we see a noticeable tendency towards their elaboration into the primary warp and woof of language. They are never more, at best, than a decorative edging to the ample, complex fabric.
6. What applies to the interjections applies with even greater force to the sound-imitative words. Such words as "whippoorwill," "to mew," "to caw" are in no sense natural sounds that man has instinctively or automatically reproduced. They are just as truly creations of the

human fancy, as anything else in language. They do not directly grow out of nature, they are suggested by it and play with it. Hence the onomatopoetic theory of the origin of speech, the theory that would explain all speech as a gradual evolution from sounds of an imitative character, really brings us no nearer to the instinctive level than is language as we know it to-day. As to the theory itself, it is scarcely more credible than its interjectional counterpart. It is true that a number of words which we do not now feel to have a sound-imitative value can be shown to have once had a phonetic form that strongly suggests their origin as imitations of natural sounds. Such is the English word "to laugh." For all that, it is quite impossible to show, nor does it seem intrinsically reasonable to suppose, that more than a negligible proportion of the elements of speech or anything at all of its formal apparatus is derivable from an onomatopoetic source. However much we may be disposed on general principles to assign a fundamental importance in the languages of primitive peoples to the imitation of natural sounds, the actual fact of the matter is that these languages show no particular preference for imitative words. Among the most primitive peoples of aboriginal America, the Athabaskan tribes of the Mackenzie River speak languages in which such words seem to be nearly or entirely absent, while they are used freely enough in languages as sophisticated as English and German. Such an instance shows how little the essential nature of speech is concerned with the mere imitation of things.

7. The way is now cleared for a serviceable definition of language. Language is a purely human and non-instinctive method of communicating ideas, emotions, and desires by means of a system of voluntarily produced symbols. These symbols are, in the first instance, auditory and they are produced by the so-called "organs of speech." There is no discernible instinctive basis in human speech as such, however much instinctive expressions and the natural environment may serve as a stimulus for the development of certain elements of speech, however much instinctive tendencies, motor and other, may give a predetermined range or mold to linguistic expression. Such human or animal communication, if "communication" it may be called, as is brought about by involuntary, instinctive cries is not, in our sense, language at all.

8. I have just referred to the "organs of speech," and it would seem at first blush that this is tantamount to an admission that speech itself

is an instinctive, biologically predetermined activity. We must not be misled by the mere term. There are, properly speaking, no organs of speech; there are only organs that are incidentally useful in the production of speech sounds. The lungs, the larynx, the palate, the nose, the tongue, the teeth, and the lips, are all so utilized, but they are no more to be thought of as primary organs of speech than are the fingers to be considered as essentially organs of piano-playing or the knees as organs of prayer. Speech is not a simple activity that is carried on by one or more organs biologically adapted to the purpose. It is an extremely complex and ever-shifting network of adjustments—in the brain, in the nervous system, and in the articulating and auditory organs—tending towards the desired end of communication. The lungs developed, roughly speaking, in connection with the necessary biological function known as breathing; the nose, as an organ of smell; the teeth, as organs useful in breaking up food before it was ready for digestion. If, then, these and other organs are being constantly utilized in speech, it is only because any organ, once existent and in so far as it is subject to voluntary control, can be utilized by man for secondary purposes. Physiologically, speech is an overlaid function, or, to be more precise, a group of overlaid functions. It gets what service it can out of organs and functions, nervous and muscular, that have come into being and are maintained for very different ends than its own.

9. It is true that physiological psychologists speak of the localization of speech in the brain. This can only mean that the sounds of speech are localized in the auditory tract of the brain, or in some circumscribed portion of it, precisely as other classes of sounds are localized; and that the motor processes involved in speech (such as the movements of the glottal cords in the larynx, the movements of the tongue required to pronounce the vowels, lip movements required to articulate certain consonants, and numerous others) are localized in the motor tract precisely as are all other impulses to special motor activities. In the same way control is lodged in the visual tract of the brain over all those processes of visual recognition involved in reading. Naturally the particular points or clusters of points of localization in the several tracts that refer to any element of language are connected in the brain by paths of association, so that the outward, or psycho-physical, aspect of language, is of a vast network of associated localizations in the brain and lower nervous tracts, the auditory localizations being without doubt the most fundamental of all for speech. However, a speech-sound localized in the brain, even when associated with the particular movements of the "speech organs" that are required to produce it, is very far from being an element of language. It must be further associated with some element or group of elements of experience, say a visual image or a class of visual images or a feeling of relation, before it has even rudimentary linguistic significance. This "element" of experience is the content or "meaning" of the linguistic unit; the associated auditory, motor, and other cerebral processes that lie immediately back of the act of speaking and the act of hearing speech are merely a complicated symbol of or signal for these "meanings," of which more anon. We see therefore at once that language as such is not and cannot be definitely localized, for it consists of a peculiar symbolic relation—physiologically an arbitrary one—between all possible elements of consciousness on the one hand and certain selected elements localized in the auditory, motor, and other cerebral and nervous tracts on the other. If language can be said to be definitely "localized" in the brain, it is only in that general and rather useless sense in which all aspects of consciousness, all human interest and activity, may be said to be "in the brain." Hence, we have no recourse but to accept language as a fully formed functional system within man's psychic or "spiritual" constitution. We cannot define it as an entity in psychophysical terms alone, however much the psychophysical basis is essential to its functioning in the individual.

10. From the physiologist's or psychologist's point of view we may seem to be making an unwarrantable abstraction in desiring to handle the subject of speech without constant and explicit reference to that basis. However, such an abstraction is justifiable. We can profitably discuss the intention, the form, and the history of speech, precisely as we discuss the nature of any other phase of human culture—say art or religion—as an institutional or cultural entity, leaving the organic and psychological mechanisms back of it as something to be taken for granted. Accordingly, it must be clearly understood that this introduction to the study of speech is not concerned with those aspects of physiology and of physiological psychology that underlie speech. Our study of language is not to be one of the genesis and operation of a concrete mechanism; it is, rather, to be an inquiry into the function and form of the arbitrary systems of symbolism that we term languages.

11. I have already pointed out that the essence of language consists in the assigning of conventional, voluntarily articulated, sounds, or of their equivalents, to the diverse elements of experience. The word "house" is not a linguistic fact if by it is meant merely the acoustic effect produced on the ear by its constituent consonants and vowels, pronounced in a certain order; nor the motor processes and tactile feelings which make up the articulation of the word; nor the visual perception on the part of the hearer of this articulation; nor the visual perception of the word "house" on the written or printed page; nor the motor processes and tactile feelings which enter into the writing of the word; nor the memory of any or all of these experiences. It is only when these, and possibly still other, associated experiences are automatically associated with the image of a house that they begin to take on the nature of a symbol, a word, an element of language. But the mere fact of such an association is not enough. One might have heard a particular word spoken in an individual house under such impressive circumstances that neither the word nor the image of the house ever recur in consciousness without the other becoming present at the same time. This type of association does not constitute speech. The association must be a purely symbolic one; in other words, the word must denote, tag off, the image, must have no other significance than to serve as a counter to refer to it whenever it is necessary or convenient to do so. Such an association, voluntary and, in a sense, arbitrary as it is, demands a considerable exercise of self-conscious attention. At least to begin with, for habit soon makes the association nearly as automatic as any and more rapid than most.

12. But we have traveled a little too fast. Were the symbol "house"— whether an auditory, motor, or visual experience or image—attached but to the single image of a particular house once seen, it might perhaps, by an indulgent criticism, be termed an element of speech, yet it is obvious at the outset that speech so constituted would have little or no value for purposes of communication. The world of our experiences must be enormously simplified and generalized before it is possible to make a symbolic inventory of all our experiences of things and relations; and this inventory is imperative before we can convey ideas. The elements of language, the symbols that ticket off experience, must therefore be associated with whole groups, delimited classes, of experience rather than with the single experiences themselves. Only so is communication possible, for the single experience lodges in an individual consciousness and is, strictly speaking, incommunicable. To be communicated it needs to be referred to a class which is tacitly accepted by the community as an identity.

Thus, the single impression which I have had of a particular house must be identified with all my other impressions of it. Further, my generalized memory or my "notion" of this house must be merged with the notions that all other individuals who have seen the house have formed of it. The particular experience that we started with has now been widened so as to embrace all possible impressions or images that sentient beings have formed or may form of the house in question. This first simplification of experience is at the bottom of a large number of elements of speech, the so-called proper nouns or names of single individuals or objects. It is, essentially, the type of simplification which underlies, or forms the crude subject of, history and art. But we cannot be content with this measure of reduction of the infinity of experience. We must cut to the bone of things, we must more or less arbitrarily throw whole masses of experience together as similar enough to warrant their being looked upon—mistakenly, but conveniently—as identical. This house and that house and thousands of other phenomena of like character are thought of as having enough in common, in spite of great and obvious differences of detail, to be classed under the same heading. In other words, the speech element "house" is the symbol, first and foremost, not of a single perception, nor even of the notion of a particular object, but of a "concept," in other words, of a convenient capsule of thought that embraces thousands of distinct experiences and that is ready to take in thousands more. If the single significant elements of speech are the symbols of concepts, the actual flow of speech may be interpreted as a record of the setting of these concepts into mutual relations.

13. The question has often been raised whether thought is possible without speech; further, if speech and thought be not but two facets of the same psychic process. The question is all the more difficult because it has been hedged about by misunderstandings. In the first place, it is well to observe that whether or not thought necessitates symbolism, that is speech, the flow of language itself is not always indicative of thought. We have seen that the typical linguistic element labels a concept. It does not follow from this that the use to which language is put is always or even mainly conceptual. We are not in ordinary life so much concerned with concepts as such as with concrete particularities and specific relations. When I say, for instance, "I had a good breakfast this morning," it is clear that I am not in the throes of laborious thought, that what I have to transmit is hardly more than a pleasurable memory symbolically rendered in the grooves of habitual expression. Each element in the sentence defines a separate concept or conceptual relation or both combined, but the sentence as a whole has no conceptual significance whatever. It is somewhat as though a dynamo capable of generating enough power to run an elevator were operated almost exclusively to feed an electric doorbell. The parallel is more suggestive than at first sight appears. Language may be looked upon as a instrument capable of running a gamut of psychic uses. Its flow not only parallels that of the inner content of consciousness, but parallels it on different levels, ranging from the state of mind that is dominated by particular images to that in which abstract concepts and their relations are alone at the focus of attention and which is ordinarily termed reasoning. Thus the outward form only of language is constant; its inner meaning, its psychic value or intensity, varies freely with attention or the selective interest of the mind, also, needless to say, with the mind's general development. From the point of view of language, thought may be defined as the highest latent or potential content of speech, the content that is obtained by interpreting each of the elements in the flow of language as possessed of its very fullest conceptual value. From this it follows at once that language and thought are not strictly coterminous. At best language can but be the outward facet of thought on the highest, most generalized, level of symbolic expression. To put our viewpoint somewhat differently, language is primarily a pre-rational function. It humbly works up to the thought that is latent in, that may eventually be read into, its classifications and its forms; it is not, as is generally but naïvely assumed, the final label put upon the finished thought.

14. Most people, asked if they can think without speech, would probably answer, "Yes, but it is not easy for me to do so. Still I know it can be done." Language is but a garment! But what if language is not so much a garment as a prepared road or groove? It is, indeed, in the highest degree likely that language is an instrument originally put to uses lower than the conceptual plane and that thought arises as a refined interpretation of its content. The product grows, in other words, with the instrument, and thought may be no more conceivable, in its genesis and daily practice, without speech than is mathematical reasoning practicable without the lever of an appropriate mathematical symbolism. No one believes that even the most difficult mathematical proposition is inherently dependent on an arbitrary set of symbols, but it is impossible to suppose that the human mind is capable of arriving at or holding such a proposition without the symbolism. The writer, for one, is strongly of the opinion that the feeling entertained by so many that they can think, or even reason, without language is an illusion. The illusion seems to be due to a number of factors. The simplest of these is the failure to distinguish between imagery and thought. As a matter of fact, no sooner do we try to put an image into conscious relation with another than we find ourselves slipping into a silent flow of words. Thought may be a natural domain apart from the artificial one of speech, but speech would seem to be the only road we know of that leads to it. A still more fruitful source of the illusive feeling that language may be dispensed with in thought is the common failure to realize that language is not identical with its auditory symbolism. The auditory symbolism may be replaced, point for point, by a motor or by a visual symbolism (many people can read, for instance, in a purely visual sense, that is, without the intermediating link of an inner flow of the auditory images that correspond to the printed or written words) or by still other, more subtle and elusive, types of transfer that are not so easy to define. Hence the contention that one thinks without language merely because he is not aware of a coexisting auditory imagery is very far indeed from being a valid one. One may go so far as to suspect that the symbolic expression of thought may in some cases run along outside the fringe of the conscious mind, so that the feeling of a free, non-linguistic stream of thought is for minds of a certain type a relatively, but only a relatively, justified one. Psycho-physically, this would mean that the auditory or equivalent visual or motor centers in the brain, together with the appropriate paths of association, that are the cerebral equivalent of speech, are touched off so lightly during the process of thought as not to rise into consciousness at all. This would be a limiting case—thought riding lightly on the submerged crests of speech, instead of jogging along with it, hand in hand. The modern psychology has shown us how powerfully symbolism is at work in the unconscious mind. It is therefore easier to understand at the present time than it would have been twenty years ago that the most rarefied thought may be but the conscious counterpart of an unconscious linguistic symbolism.

15. One word more as to the relation between language and thought. The point of view that we have developed does not by any means preclude the possibility of the growth of speech being in a high degree dependent on the development of thought. We may assume that language arose pre-rationally—just how and on what precise level of mental activity we do not know—but we must not imagine that a highly developed system of speech symbols worked itself out before the genesis of distinct concepts and of thinking, the handling of concepts. We must rather imagine that thought processes set in, as a kind of psychic overflow, almost at the beginning of linguistic expression; further, that the concept, once defined, necessarily reacted on the life of its linguistic symbol, encouraging further linguistic growth. We see this complex process of the interaction of language and thought actually taking place under our eyes. The instrument makes possible the product, the product refines the instrument. The birth of a new concept is invariably foreshadowed by a more or less strained or extended use of old linguistic material; the concept does not attain to individual and independent life until it has found a distinctive linguistic embodiment. In most cases the new symbol is but a thing wrought from linguistic material already in existence in ways mapped out by crushingly despotic precedents. As soon as the word is at hand, we instinctively feel, with something of a sigh of relief, that the concept is ours for the handling. Not until we own the symbol do we feel that we hold a key to the immediate knowledge or understanding of the concept. Would we be so ready to die for "liberty," to struggle for "ideals," if the words themselves were not ringing within us? And the word, as we know, is not only a key; it may also be a fetter.

16. Language is primarily an auditory system of symbols. In so far as it is articulated it is also a motor system, but the motor aspect of speech is clearly secondary to the auditory. In normal individuals the impulse to speech first takes effect in the sphere of auditory imagery and is then transmitted to the motor nerves that control the organs of speech. The motor processes and the accompanying motor feelings are not, however, the end, the final resting point. They are merely a means and a control leading to auditory perception in both speaker and hearer. Communication, which is the very object of speech, is successfully effected only when the hearer's auditory perceptions are translated into the appropriate and intended flow of imagery or thought or both combined. Hence the cycle of speech, in so far as we may look upon it as a purely external instrument, begins and ends in the realm

of sounds. The concordance between the initial auditory imagery and the final auditory perceptions is the social seal or warrant of the successful issue of the process. As we have already seen, the typical course of this process may undergo endless modifications or transfers into equivalent systems without thereby losing its essential formal characteristics.

17. The most important of these modifications is the abbreviation of the speech process involved in thinking. This has doubtless many forms, according to the structural or functional peculiarities of the individual mind. The least modified form is that known as "talking to one's self" or "thinking aloud." Here the speaker and the hearer are identified in a single person, who may be said to communicate with himself. More significant is the still further abbreviated form in which the sounds of speech are not articulated at all. To this belong all the varieties of silent speech and of normal thinking. The auditory centers alone may be excited; or the impulse to linguistic expression may be communicated as well to the motor nerves that communicate with the organs of speech but be inhibited either in the muscles of these organs or at some point in the motor nerves themselves; or, possibly, the auditory centers may be only slightly, if at all, affected, the speech process manifesting itself directly in the motor sphere. There must be still other types of abbreviation. How common is the excitation of the motor nerves in silent speech, in which no audible or visible articulations result, is shown by the frequent experience of fatigue in the speech organs, particularly in the larynx, after unusually stimulating reading or intensive thinking.

18. All the modifications so far considered are directly patterned on the typical process of normal speech. Of very great interest and importance is the possibility of transferring the whole system of speech symbolism into other terms than those that are involved in the typical process. This process, as we have seen, is a matter of sounds and of movements intended to produce these sounds. The sense of vision is not brought into play. But let us suppose that one not only hears the articulated sounds but sees the articulations themselves as they are being executed by the speaker. Clearly, if one can only gain a sufficiently high degree of adroitness in perceiving these movements of the speech organs, the way is opened for a new type of speech symbolism —that in which the sound is replaced by the visual image of the articu-

lations that correspond to the sound. This sort of system has no great value for most of us because we are already possessed of the auditory-motor system of which it is at best but an imperfect translation, not all the articulations being visible to the eye. However, it is well known what excellent use deaf-mutes can make of "reading from the lips" as a subsidiary method of apprehending speech. The most important of all visual speech symbolisms is, of course, that of the written or printed word, to which, on the motor side, corresponds the system of delicately adjusted movements which result in the writing or typewriting or other graphic method of recording speech. The significant feature for our recognition in these new types of symbolism, apart from the fact that they are no longer a by-product of normal speech itself, is that each element (letter or written word) in the system corresponds to a specific element (sound or sound-group or spoken word) in the primary system. Written language is thus a point-to-point equivalence, to borrow a mathematical phrase, to its spoken counterpart. The written forms are secondary symbols of the spoken ones—symbols of symbols—yet so close is the correspondence that they may, not only in theory but in the actual practice of certain eye-readers and, possibly, in certain types of thinking, be entirely substituted for the spoken ones. Yet the auditory-motor associations are probably always latent at the least, that is, they are unconsciously brought into play. Even those who read and think without the slightest use of sound imagery are, at last analysis, dependent on it. They are merely handling the circulating medium, the money, of visual symbols as a convenient substitute for the economic goods and services of the fundamental auditory symbols.

19. The possibilities of linguistic transfer are practically unlimited. A familiar example is the Morse telegraph code, in which the letters of written speech are represented by a conventionally fixed sequence of longer or shorter ticks. Here the transfer takes place from the written word rather than directly from the sounds of spoken speech. The letter of the telegraph code is thus a symbol of a symbol of a symbol. It does not, of course, in the least follow that the skilled operator, in order to arrive at an understanding of a telegraphic message, needs to transpose the individual sequence of ticks into a visual image of the word before he experiences its normal auditory image. The precise method of reading off speech from the telegraphic communication undoubtedly varies widely with the individual. It is even conceivable, if not exactly likely, that certain operators may have learned to think directly, so far as the purely conscious part of the process of thought is concerned, in terms of the tick-auditory symbolism or, if they happen to have a strong natural bent toward motor symbolism, in terms of the correlated tactile-motor symbolism developed in the sending of telegraphic messages.

20. Still another interesting group of transfers are the different gesture languages, developed for the use of deaf-mutes, of Trappist monks vowed to perpetual silence, or of communicating parties that are within seeing distance of each other but are out of earshot. Some of these systems are one-to-one equivalences of the normal system of speech; others, like military gesture-symbolism or the gesture language of the Plains Indians of North America (understood by tribes of mutually unintelligible forms of speech) are imperfect transfers, limiting themselves to the rendering of such grosser speech elements as are an imperative minimum under difficult circumstances. In these latter systems, as in such still more imperfect symbolisms as those used at sea or in the woods, it may be contended that language no longer properly plays a part but that the ideas are directly conveyed by an utterly unrelated symbolic process or by a quasi-instinctive imitativeness. Such an interpretation would be erroneous. The intelligibility of these vaguer symbolisms can hardly be due to anything but their automatic and silent translation into the terms of a fuller flow of speech.

21. We shall no doubt conclude that all voluntary communication of ideas, aside from normal speech, is either a transfer, direct or indirect, from the typical symbolism of language as spoken and heard or, at the least, involves the intermediary of truly linguistic symbolism. This is a fact of the highest importance. Auditory imagery and the correlated motor imagery leading to articulation are, by whatever devious ways we follow the process, the historic fountain-head of all speech and of all thinking. One other point is of still greater importance. The ease with which speech symbolism can be transferred from one sense to another, from technique to technique, itself indicates that the mere sounds of speech are not the essential fact of language, which lies rather in the classification, in the formal patterning, and in the relating of concepts. Once more, language, as a structure, is on its inner face the mold of thought. It is this abstracted language, rather more than the physical facts of speech, that is to concern us in our inquiry.

22. There is no more striking general fact about language than its universality. One may argue as to whether a particular tribe engages in activities that are worthy of the name of religion or of art, but we know of no people that is not possessed of a fully developed language. The lowliest South African Bushman speaks in the forms of a rich symbolic system that is in essence perfectly comparable to the speech of the cultivated Frenchman. It goes without saying that the more abstract concepts are not nearly so plentifully represented in the language of the savage, nor is there the rich terminology and the finer definition of nuances that reflect the higher culture. Yet the sort of linguistic development that parallels the historic growth of culture and which, in its later stages, we associate with literature is, at best, but a superficial thing. The fundamental groundwork of language— the development of a clear-cut phonetic system, the specific association of speech elements with concepts, and the delicate provision for the formal expression of all manner of relations—all this meets us rigidly perfected and systematized in every language known to us. Many primitive languages have a formal richness, a latent luxuriance of expression, that eclipses anything known to the languages of modern civilization. Even in the mere matter of the inventory of speech the layman must be prepared for strange suprises. Popular statements as to the extreme poverty of expression to which primitive languages are doomed are simply myths. Scarcely less impressive than the universality of speech is its almost incredible diversity. Those of us that have studied French or German, or, better yet, Latin or Greek, know in what varied forms a thought may run. The formal divergences between the English plan and the Latin plan, however, are comparatively slight in the perspective of what we know of more exotic linguistic patterns. The universality and the diversity of speech lead to a significant inference. We are forced to believe that language is an immensely ancient heritage of the human race, whether or not all forms of speech are the historical outgrowth of a single pristine form. It is doubtful if any other cultural asset of man, be it the art of drilling for fire or of chipping stone, may lay claim to a greater age. I am inclined to believe that it antedated even the lowliest developments

of material culture, that these developments, in fact, were not strictly possible until language, the tool of significant expression, had itself taken shape.

Meanwhile the desire to express myself grew. The few signs I used became less and less adequate, and my failures to make myself understood were invariably followed by outbursts of passion. I felt as if invisible hands were holding me, and I made frantic efforts to free myself.

. . . my teacher . . . brought me my hat, and I knew I was going out into the warm sunshine. This thought, if a wordless sensation may be called a thought, made me hop and skip with pleasure.

We walked down the path to the well-house. . . . Some one was drawing water and my teacher placed my hand under the spout. As the cool stream gushed over one hand she spelled into the other the word *water,* first slowly, then rapidly. I stood still, my whole attention fixed upon the motions of her fingers. Suddenly I felt a misty consciousness as of something forgotten—a thrill of returning thought; and somehow the mystery of language was revealed to me. I knew then that "w-a-t-e-r" meant the wonderful cool something that was flowing over my hand. That living word awakened my soul, gave it light, hope, joy, set it free! . . . I left the well-house eager to learn. Everything had a name, and each name gave birth to a new thought. As we returned to the house every object which I touched seemed to quiver with life.

Helen Keller,

The Story of My Life

Different maps of a given territory are approximations of reality, and more. They also reveal the map-makers themselves: what interested them, what they did and did not notice, the multitude of interpretations and categorizations of reality which, both consciously and unconsciously, guided them as they worked. In a similar way the documents from various stages of the development of a language reveal their subjects and the culture of their writers. In the following excerpt from THE GROWTH AND STRUCTURE OF THE ENGLISH LANGUAGE Otto Jespersen describes important changes in the language of Britain which followed its fifth century invasion and settlement by German tribes and the slightly later Christianization of its inhabitants. Without these two crucial events, as Jespersen makes clear, the language we speak would be basically quite different. Are other historical developments changing our language today? Will any of them result in transformations as major as those Jespersen describes?

The Founding of English

Otto Jespersen

We now come to the first of those important historical events which have materially influenced the English language, namely the settlement of Britain by Germanic tribes. The other events of paramount importance, which we shall have to deal with in succession, are the Scandinavian invasion, the Norman conquest, and the revival of learning. A future historian will certainly add the spreading of the English

From *The Growth and Structure of the English Language* by Otto Jespersen, by permission of Appleton-Century, affiliate of Meredith Press. Copyright 1927 by D. Appleton & Company.

language in America, Australia, and South Africa. But none of these can compare in significance with the first conquest of England by the English, an event which was, perhaps, fraught with greater consequences for the future of the world in general than anything else in history. The more is the pity that we know so very little either of the people who came over or of the state of things they found in the country they invaded. We do not know exactly *when* the invasion began; the date usually given is 449, but Bede, on whose authority this date rests, wrote about three hundred years later, and much may have been forgotten in so long a period. Many considerations seem to make it more advisable to give a rather earlier date; however, as we must imagine that the invaders did not come all at once, but that the settlement took up a comparatively long period during which new hordes were continually arriving, the question of date is of no great consequence, and we are probably on the safe side if we say that after a long series of Germanic invasions the country was practically in their power in the latter half of the fifth century.

2. *Who* were the invaders, and where did they come from? This, too, has been a point of controversy. According to Bede, the invaders belonged to the three tribes of Angles, Saxons, and Jutes; and linguistic history corroborates his statement in so far as we have really three dialects, or groups of dialects: the Anglian dialects in the North with two subdivisions, Northumbrian and Mercian, the Saxon dialects in the greater part of the South, the most important of which was the dialect of Wessex (West-Saxon), and the Kentish dialect, Kent having been, according to tradition, settled by the Jutes.

3. What language or what languages did the settlers find on their arrival in Britain? The original population was Celtic; but what about the Roman conquest? The Romans had been masters of the country for centuries; had they not succeeded in making the native population learn Latin as they had succeeded in Spain and Gaul? Some years ago Pogatscher took up the view that they had succeeded, and that the Angles and Saxons found a Brito-Roman dialect in full vigour. But this view was very strongly attacked, and Pogatscher, in a subsequent article, had to withdraw his previous theory, if not completely, yet to a great extent, so that he no longer maintains that Latin ever was the *national* language of Britain, though he does not go the length of saying with Loth that the Latin language disappeared from Britain when the Roman troops were withdrawn. The possibility is left that

while people in the country spoke Celtic, the inhabitants of the towns spoke Latin or that some of them did. However this may be, the fact remains that the English found on their arrival a population speaking a different language from their own. Did that, then, affect their own language, and in what manner and to what extent?

4. The net result of modern investigation seems to be that (apart from numerous place-names) not quite a dozen words did pass over into English from the British aborigines (among them are *ass, bannock, binn, brock*). How may we account for this very small number of loans? Sweet says the reason was that 'the Britons themselves were to a great extent Romanized,' a theory which we seem bound to abandon now (see above). Are we to account for it, as some writers would, from the unscrupulous character of the conquest, the English having killed all those Britons who did not run away into the mountainous districts? The supposition of wholesale slaughter is not, however, necessary, for a thorough consideration of the general conditions under which borrowings from one language by another take place will give us a clue to the mystery. And as the whole history of the English language may be described from one point of view as one chain of borrowings, it will be as well at the outset to give a little thought to this general question.

5. The whole theory about mixed languages turns upon this formula: it is not the foreign language a nation learns that turns into a mixed language, but its own native language becomes mixed under the influence of the foreign language. When we try to learn and talk a foreign language we do not intermix it with words taken from our own language; our endeavour will always be to speak the other language as purely as possible, generally we are painfully conscious of every native word that we use in the middle of phrases framed in the other tongue. But what we thus avoid in speaking a foreign language we very often do in our own. An illustration may be taken from Germany in the eighteenth century. It was then the height of fashion to imitate everything French, and Frederick the Great prided himself on speaking and writing good French. In his French writings one finds not a single German word, but whenever he wrote German, French words and phrases in the middle of German sentences abounded, for French was considered more refined, more *distingué*. Similarly, in the last remains of Cornish, the extinct Celtic language of Cornwall, numerous English loan-words occur, but the English did not mix any

Cornish words with their own language, and the inhabitants of Cornwall themselves, whose native language was Cornish, would naturally
avoid Cornish words when talking English, because in the first place
English was considered the superior tongue, the language of culture
and civilization, and second, the English would not understand Cornish words. Similarly in the Brittany of to-day, people will interlard
their Breton talk with French words, while their French is pure, without any Breton words. We now see why so few Celtic words were
taken over into English. There was nothing to induce the ruling
classes to learn the language of the inferior natives; it could never be
fashionable for them to show an acquaintance with that despised
tongue by using now and then a Celtic word. On the other hand, the
Celt would have to learn the language of his masters, and learn it
well; he could not think of addressing his superiors in his own unintelligible gibberish, and if the first generation did not learn good English,
the second or third would, while the influence they themselves exer-
cised on English would be infinitesimal. There can be no doubt that
this theory is in the main correct, though we shall, perhaps, later on
see instances where it holds good only with some qualification. At
any rate we need look for no other explanation of the fewness of Celtic
words in English.

6. About 600 A. D. England was christianized, and the conversion
had far-reaching linguistic consequences. We have no literary remains of the pre-Christian period, but in the great epic of *Beowulf*
we see a strange mixture of pagan and Christian elements. It took a
long time thoroughly to assimilate the new doctrine, and, in fact,
much of the old heathendom survives to this day in the shape of
numerous superstitions. On the other hand, we must not suppose that
people were wholly unacquainted with Christianity before they were
actually converted, and linguistic evidence points to their knowing,
and having had names for, the most striking Christian phenomena
centuries before they became Christians themselves. One of the earliest loan-words belonging to this sphere is *church*, OE. *cirice, cyrice,*
ultimately from Greek *kuriakón* '(house) of the Lord' or rather the
plural *kuriaká*. It has been well remarked that 'it is by no means necessary that there should have been a single *kirika* in Germany itself;
from 313 onwards, Christian churches with their sacred vessels and
ornaments were well-known objects of pillage to the German invaders
of the Empire: if the first with which these made acquaintance, wher-

ever situated, were called *kuriaká*, it would be quite sufficient to account for their familiarity with the word.' They knew this word so
well that when they became Christians they did not adopt the word
universally used in the Latin church and in the Romance languages
(*ecclesia, église, chiesa,* etc.), and the English even extended the
signification of the word *church* from the building to the congrega-
tion, the whole body of Christians.

7. The number of new ideas and things introduced with Christianity
was very considerable, and it is interesting to note how the English
managed to express them in their language. In the first place they
adopted a great many foreign words together with the ideas. Such
words are *apostle* OE. *apostol, disciple* OF. *discipul,* which has been
more of an ecclesiastical word in English than in other languages,
where it has the wider Latin sense of 'pupil' or 'scholar,' while in English it is more or less limited to the twelve Disciples of Jesus or to
similar applications. Further, the names of the whole scale of digni-
taries of the church, from the *Pope,* OE. *papa,* downwards through
archbishop OE. *ercebiscop, bishop* OE. *biscop,* to *priest* OE. *preost;*
so also *monk* OE. *munuc, nun* OE. *nunna* with *provost* OE. *prafost*
(præpositus) and *profost* (propositus), *abbot* OE. *abbod* (*d* from Romance form) and the feminine OE. *abbudisse.* Here belong also such
obsolete words as *sacerd* 'priest,' *canonic* 'canon,' *decan* 'dean,' *ancor*
or *ancra* 'hermit' (Lat. *anachoreta*). To these names of persons must be
added not a few names of things, such as *shrine* OE. *scrin* (scrinium),
cowl OE. *cugele* (cuculla), *pall* OE. *pœll* or *pell* (pallium); *regol* or
reogol '(monastic) rule,' *capitul* 'chapter,' *mœsse* 'mass,' and *offrian,* in
Old English used only in the sense of 'sacrificing, bringing an offer-
ing'; the modern usage is 'he offered his friend a seat and a cigar' is
later and from the French.

8. It is worth noting that most of these loans were short words that
tallied perfectly well with the native words and were easily inflected
and treated in every respect like these; the composition of the longest
of them *ercebiscop,* was felt quite naturally as a native one. Such long
words as *discipul* or *capitul,* or as *exorcista* and *acolitus,* which are
also found, never became popular words; and *anachoreta* only became popular when it had been shortened to the convenient *ancor.*

9. The chief interest in this chapter of linguistic history does not, however, to my mind concern those words that were adopted, but those
that were not. It is not astonishing that the English should have learnt

some Latin words connected with the new faith, but it is astonishing, especially in the light of what later generations did, that they should have utilized the resources of their own language to so great an extent as was actually the case. This was done in three ways: by forming new words from the foreign loans by means of native affixes, by modifying the sense of existing English words, and finally by framing new words from native stems.

10. At that period the English were not shy of affixing native endings to foreign words; thus we have a great many words in -*had* (mod. -*hood*): *preosthad* 'priesthood,' *clerichad, sacerdhad, biscophad* 'episcopate,' etc.; also such compounds as *biscopsetl* 'episcopal see,' *biscopscir* 'diocese,' and with the same ending *profostscir* 'provostship' and the interesting *scriftscir* 'parish, confessor's district' from *scrift* 'confession,' a derivative of *scrifan (shrive)* from Lat. *scribere* in the sense 'impose penance, hear confession.' Note also such words as *cristendom* 'Christendom, Christianity' (also *cristnes*), and *cristnian* 'christen' or rather 'prepare a candidate for baptism' and *biscopian* 'confirm' with the noun *biscepung* 'confirmation.'

11. Existing native words were largely turned to account to express Christian ideas, the sense only being more or less modified. Foremost among these must be mentioned the word *God*. Other words belonging to the same class and surviving to this day are *sin* OE. *synn, tithe* OE. *teoða,* the old ordinal for 'tenth'; *easter* OE., *eastron* was the name of an old pagan spring festival, called after Austro, a goddess of spring. Most of the native words adapted to Christian usage have since been superseded by terms taken from Latin or French. Where we now say *saint* from the French, the old word was *halig* (mod. *holy*), preserved in *All-hallows-day* and *Allhallowe'en;* the Lat. *sanct* was very rarely used.

12. This second class is not always easily distinguished from the third, or those words that had not previously existed but were now framed out of existing native speech-material to express ideas foreign to the pagan world. Word-composition and other formative processes were resorted to, and in some instances the new terms were simply fitted together from translations of the component parts of the Greek or Latin word they were intended to render, as when Greek *euaggélion* was rendered *gōd-spell* (good-spell, afterwards with shortening of the first vowel *godspell*, which was often taken to be the 'spell' or message of God), mod. *gospel;* thence *godspellere* where now the foreign word *evangelist* is used. *Heathen*, OE. *hǽðen*, according to the generally accepted theory, is derived from *hǽþ* 'heath' in close imitation of Latin *paganus* from *pagus* 'a country district'. *Cf.* also *þrynnes* or *þrines* ('three-ness') for *trinity*.

13. But in most cases we have no such literal rendering of a foreign term, but excellent words devised exactly as if the framers of them had never heard of any foreign expression for the same conception—as, perhaps, indeed, in some instances they had not. Some of these display not a little ingenuity. The scribes and Pharisees of the New Testament were called *boceras* (from *boc* book) and *sunder-halgan* (from *sundor* 'apart, asunder, separate'); in the north the latter were also called *ǽlarwas* 'teachers of the Law' or *ǽldo* 'elders.' A patriarch was called *heahfǽder* 'high-father' or *eald-fǽder* 'old-father'; the three Magi were called *tungol-witegan* from *tungol* 'star,' and *witega* 'wise man.' To 'baptize' was expressed by *dyppan* 'dip' (*cf.* German *taufen*, Dan. *døbe*) or more often by *fulwian* (from *ful-wihan* 'to consecrate completely'); 'baptism' by *fulwiht* or, the last syllable being phonetically obscured, *fulluht*, and John the Baptist was called *Johannes se fulluhtere*.

14. The power and boldness of these numerous native formations can, perhaps, be best appreciated if we go through the principal compounds of *God: godbot* 'atonement made to the church,' *godcund* 'divine, religious, sacred,' *godcundnes* 'divinity, sacred office,' *godferht* 'pious,' *godgield* 'idol,' *godgimm* 'divine gem,' *godhad* 'divine nature,' *godmǽgen* 'divinity,' *godscyld* 'impiety,' *godscyldig* 'impious,' *godsibb* 'sponsor,' *godsibbrǽden* 'sponsorial obligations,' *godspelbodung* 'gospel-preaching,' *godspellere* 'evangelist,' *godspellian* 'preach the gospel,' *godspellisc* 'evangelical,' *godspeltraht* 'gospel-commentary,' *godsprǽce* 'oracle,' *godsunu* 'godson,' *godþrymm* 'divine majesty,' *godwrǽc* 'impious,' *godwrǽcnes* 'impriety.' Such a list as this, with the modern translations, shows the gulf between the old system of nomenclature, where everything was native and, therefore, easily understood by even the most uneducated, and the modern system, where with few exceptions classical roots serve to express even simple ideas; observe that although *gospel* has been retained, the easy secondary words derived from it have given way to learned formations. Nor was it only religious terms that were devised in this way; for Christianity brought with it also some acquaintance with the higher intellectual achievements in other domains, and we find such scientific terms as *lœce-crœft* 'leech-craft' for medicine, *tungol-œ* ('star-law') for astronomy, *efnniht* for equinox, *sun-stede* and *sungihte* for solstice, *sunfolgend* (sunfollower) for heliotrope, *tid* 'tide' and *gemet* 'measure' for tense and mood in grammar, *foresetnes* for preposition, etc., in short a number of scientific expressions of native origin, such as is equalled among the Germanic languages in Icelandic only.

15. If now we ask, why did not the Anglo-Saxons adopt more of the ready-made Latin or Greek words, it is easy to see that the conditions here are quite different from those mentioned above when we asked a similar question with regard to Celtic. There we had a real race-mixture, where people speaking two different languages were living in actual contact in the same country. Here we have no Latin-speaking nation or community in actual intercourse with the English; and though we must suppose that there was a certain mouth-to-mouth influence from missionaries which might familiarize part of the English nation with some of the specifically Christian words, these were certainly at first introduced in far greater number through the medium of writing, exactly as is the case with Latin and Greek importations in recent times. Why, then, do we see such a difference between the practice of that remote period and our own time? One of the reasons seems obviously to be that people then did not know so much Latin as they learnt later, so that these learned words, if introduced, would not have been understood. We have it on King Alfred's authority that in the time immediately preceding his own reign 'there were very few on this side of the Humber who could understand their (Latin) rituals in English, or translate a letter from Latin into English, and I believe that there were not many beyond the Humber. There were so few of them that I cannot remember a single one south of the Thames when I came to the throne . . . and there was also a great multitude of God's servants, but they had very little knowledge of the books, for they could not understand anything of them, because they were not writ-regrets, when 'the sacred orders were zealous in teaching and learn-ten in their language.' And even in the previous period which Alfred ing,' and when, as we know from Bede and other sources, Latin and Greek studies were pursued successfully in England, we may be sure that the percentage of those who would have understood the learned words, had they been adopted into English, was not large. There was, therefore, good reason for devising as many popular words as possible. However, the manner in which our question was put was not, perhaps, quite fair, for we seemed to presuppose that it would be natural for a nation to adopt as many foreign terms as its linguistic digestion would admit, and that it would be matter for surprise if a language had fewer foreign elements than Modern English. But on the contrary, it is rather the natural thing for a language to utilize its own resources before drawing on other languages. The Anglo-Saxon principle of adopting only such words as were easily assimilated with the native vocabulary, for the most part names of concrete things, and of turning to the greatest possible account native words and roots, especially for abstract notions,—that principle may be taken as a symptom of a healthful condition of a language and a nation; witness Greek, where we have the most flourishing and vigorous growth of abstract and other scientifically serviceable terms on a native basis that the world has ever seen, and where the highest development of intellectual and artistic activity went hand in hand with the most extensive creation of indigenous words and an extremely limited importation of words from abroad. It is not, then, the Old English system of utilizing the vernacular stock of words, but the modern system of neglecting the native and borrowing from a foreign vocabulary that has to be accounted for as something out of the natural state of things.

Du ure faeder þe eart on heofenu seo þin nama geholgod. Cume ðin rice. Seo ðin wylla on eorðan swa swa on heofenum. Syle us to-daeg urne daeghwamlican hlaf. And forgyf us ure gyltas, swa swa we forgyfað ðam þe wið us agyltaþ. And ne laed þu na us on costnunge, ac alys us fram yfele. Sy hit swa.

Aelfric's Homilies, late 10th C.

Our fadir þat art in hevenes, halwid be þi name; þi reume or kyngdom come to þe. Be þi wille don in herþe as it is doun in hevene. ȝeve to us to-day oure eche dayes bred. And forȝeve to us oure dettis, þat is oure synnys, as we forȝeven tu oure dettouris, þat is to men þat han synned in us. And lede us not in-to temptacioun, but delyvere us from evyl. Amen, so be it.

late 14th C. manuscript

Our father, whiche arte in heaven, hallowed by thy name. Thy kyngdom come. Thy wyll be done in earth as it is in heaven. Geve us this daye oure dayly bread. And forgeve us oure trespasses, as we forgeve them that trespasse agaynst us. And leade us not into temptacioun. But deliver us from evell. Amen.

Book of Common Prayer, 1552

Each language, according to Stephen Ullmann, is "a prism, unique in structure, through which we view the world and which refracts and analyses our experiences in its own particular way." This sounds innocent until one considers that Ullmann has partially assigned to language the ORGANIZATION of thought and the ANALYSIS of experience. Language may limit us in ways we seldom imagine by effectively doing some of our thinking for us. In the following essay Ullmann considers several examples of this sometimes neglected aspect of language, and wonders if language may even be an inadequate medium of expression.

The Prism of Language

Stephen Ullmann

Language is so much a part of our lives that we seldom stop to think about it. We take it for granted that our words are mere passive tools, means of self-expression and of communication. But there is another way of looking at language. Words certainly are the vehicles of our thoughts, but they may be far more than that: they may acquire an influence of their own, shaping and pre-determining our processes of thinking and our whole outlook.

From *The Listener*, LII, July 22, 1954, No. 1325. Reprinted by permission of the author.

2. At first sight, this picture of language as an active force may seem strange and far-fetched. For most people, words are something purely external, the mere 'dress of thought', as Dr. Johnson put it; how could they influence the working of our minds? And yet some of our everyday experiences should warn us that language can play a more active part. When we translate from one idiom to another, our thoughts are apt to suffer a subtle transformation, a kind of sea-change; and if one tries to re-translate the text into the original, one is surprised to see how far it has moved from its starting point. The translator's task is even more complicated if the two languages belong to different civilisations; there can be no exact correspondence between the vocabulary of an Englishman and a Chinese.

3. The problem becomes almost insoluble when one has to translate from a civilised into an uncivilised language. We come up at once against a fundamental discrepancy between our own speech-habits and those of primitive races. Missionaries and others have noted, time and again, that these races have a multiplicity of concrete, specialised terms but are remarkably poor in generic ones. They would have, for example, separate names for each variety of tree, but no general word for 'tree' itself. Their verbs show the same pattern: there is no single term for the act of 'cutting' but a number of expressions for cutting various objects. In some cases the missionaries may have failed to elicit the right word, but the general tendency stands out clearly, and it also fits in with what we know about the history of our own languages.

4. How far does this affect the mental development of the individual native speaker? It means that he is born with a language which has no provision for general ideas, which does not help him in classifying his impressions and experiences. He could, no doubt, develop higher concepts of his own if the need arose, but this would cost him an effort which more fortunate speakers, born with a more differentiated linguistic equipment, need not make: the work has been done for them by their mother tongue, or rather by previous generations whose accumulated experience is deposited in the language.

5. It could be argued that the predominance of particular terms may be due not to faulty powers of abstraction but to biological necessity. The Lapps of the arctic regions have no general term for 'snow', only a number of special names for each state and form of it: snow is so important a factor in their lives that they have to specify its various aspects. The fact remains that they have failed to take the next step, that of subordinating these aspects to the higher concept of snow; and this failure has been perpetuated by their language. There is a curious form of reciprocity between language and thought: language reflects our thoughts but it also reacts upon them, by crystallising and preserving the picture of the world which they build up.

6. The savage with his over-concrete vocabulary has a strange parallel in the civilised speaker who has lost the full power of speech. Experiments on patients suffering from head wounds during and after the first world war have revealed some significant facts about the interaction of words and thought. Such injuries may affect any element of speech: elocution, grammar, comprehension, and even the very basis of language, the connection between words and their meanings. One of these patients was suffering from a rare condition: he had forgotten the names of colours. In some ways he behaved as if he were colour blind; yet his physical sense of colour was unimpaired. In one experiment he was faced with a number of coloured threads, all different in shade, and was asked to pick out those belonging to the same colour. But he found this task meaningless: to him, the various shades of green and blue were totally different as he had no term for, and therefore no concept of, 'greenness' or 'blueness' to which they could be subordinated. Language had classified the endless variety of colours into a few cardinal types; now that this key had been lost, the man-made order relapsed into chaos.

7. But we need not go to the Australian bushmen or to the nerve specialist to study the impact of language on thought. Our own languages contain ample evidence of the same influence. In each of them, the raw material of experience is analysed, docketed, and arranged in a unique way; every vocabulary embodies a scale of values and a philosophy of life. The concepts which it comprises have been elaborated and organised by preceding generations; the child assimilates them with the mother tongue and accepts them as the natural way of viewing the world, though he may later on modify some detail in the light of his own experience. Even the impressions reaching us through our senses have to be sifted and organised by language; and each language will organise them in its own way. Take the problem of colours. To us, our own system of distinctions seems the only natural one; but in the spectrum itself there are no boundaries: each language can divide it into as many, or as few, sections as it chooses.

When it was first realised that some of our shades of colour were absent from the Homeric epics, it was suggested that Homer must have been colour blind. Later on, the whole of classical antiquity was included in the same diagnosis. And, indeed, the Greeks and the Romans had a simpler system than ours. But neither the ancient nor the modern scheme can be held up as the only valid one: they are merely two of the many possible attempts at organising what nature had left unorganised.

Labelling Important Qualities

8. Our intellectual and moral concepts are even more language-bound than our vision of the physical world. Every community will single out and label those qualities which it considers important, whereas other features will remain unnamed and therefore undifferentiated. In medieval society, cleverness as such was not recognised as an independent quality; at the same time, courtly and non-courtly, chivalric and non-chivalric skill were systematically distinguished and provided with separate names. Once again, we see the reciprocity of relations between language and thought. The vocabulary reflects a certain hierarchy of values, but it also hardens it and hands it down to successive generations. Its action is essentially conservative; it is one of the most powerful factors building up traditions and ensuring continuity.

9. In some cases, even the presence or absence of a single word may be significant, though here we should be aware of hasty and biased interpretation. Take the case of the German word *Schadenfreude*, 'malicious joy', which has no exact equivalent in English or French. Should one infer from this, as has been done, that Germans suffer more from this vice than do other nations? One could maintain with equal justification that they are more likely to be immune from it, as the very existence of the word puts them on their guard. Be that as it may, it is a fact that the young German is born with a linguistic medium where malicious joy is identified and given a name of its own, whereas elsewhere it remains in the limbo of anonymity.

10. Various analogies have been suggested to bring out the essential features of the influence of language on thought. Some thinkers are obsessed by a kind of linguistic claustrophobia: they conjure up a dramatic picture of man trapped between the walls of his mother tongue. It is perhaps more appropriate to visualise each language as

a prism, unique in structure, through which we view the world and which refracts and analyses our experiences in its own particular way. This is seen most clearly in the vocabulary, but grammatical structure tells a similar story. The impact of grammatical conventions on the human mind is even more far-reaching than that of single words. Pronouns of address are an example in point. Most languages have two or more such pronouns, which will be used according to degree of intimacy, social status, and other factors. English, however, differs from the rest: since the elimination of 'thou' in the late Middle Ages, there is no possibility of choice. This may lead occasionally to awkward ambiguities, but the risk is more than offset by the amount of snobbery and arrogance, of inhibitions and inferiority complexes, which the English-speaking world has been spared thanks to this simple device.

11. Other grammatical features reach down to deeper layers of our consciousness. Even the experience of time has a linguistic dimension. Modern physics has taught us that time is relative, and this applies also to its grammatical expression. The number and nature of tense distinctions differs from one language to another; some idioms, especially the Slavonic ones, are actually less interested in time proper than in the complete or incomplete nature of a given action. The late Professor Entwistle has given an interesting analysis of this peculiarity:

> We are concerned with an attitude of mind in which the continuance or completion of some action is of more importance than its reference to past, present, or future time. This emphasis may be connected with the agricultural occupation of most Slavs as contrasted with the urban precision imposed on westerners. . . . The preference we westerners have for tense is probably due partly to the influence of European modes of life, which depend on the clock, and not, like the agricultural, on the completion of operations.

One may wonder whether recent industrial progress in the Slav world will result in some modification of their time scale. Meanwhile, the time-perspective of the mother tongue is bound to have an influence on the individual speaker's conception of time.

12. The characteristic features of a language may thus tell us a great deal about national psychology. Particularly instructive in this respect are the habitual patterns of word-order which determine the channels along which our thoughts will flow. The vast majority of English and French sentences are built on a rigid pattern: the sequence subject—verb—object, as in 'Peter sees Paul'. This sequence may be regarded as inherently logical: first, we state the subject of the utterance, that which we are talking about; then we say something about it; finally, we may add any further details required. There is little possibility of departing from this arrangement, as English and French words are uninflected and their position alone marks their role in the sentence. In inflected languages, such as German, there will be a wider margin, and the logical scheme may be superseded by emphasis and other considerations. There is also another significant difference. While English and French sentences proceed in a straight line, German syntax prefers elaborate constructions which have been described as 'incapsulating': they are like boxes fitted into one another. A prefix, for example, will be detached from its verb and relegated to the very end of the sentence; it is as if we said in English: 'An epidemic broke last year in England out'. This requires a certain amount of planning in which some people may detect a characteristic trait of the German mind. It would be idle to speculate as to which system is preferable: both involve some effort and discipline, though each in its own way.

13. Some modern thinkers are haunted by the fear that many philosophical problems are pseudo-problems generated by the structure of our languages. One often hears statements of this type: 'If Aristotle had spoken Chinese or Dacotan, he would have had to adopt an entirely different logic'. But it still has to be shown in detail how linguistic structure can influence philosophical structure. Other philosophers are more concerned with those features of language which may distort or confuse our thoughts. Abstractions have been singled out for special attention, and we are constantly warned against the habit of setting up our 'isms' and other abstract formations as real entities, and of assuming that where there is a label there must necessarily be some reality behind it. The very ease with which some languages, in particular German, are able to coin an unlimited number of abstract terms may thus become a potential danger to clear thinking.

14. Ambiguities are also denounced by the philosopher, though they may be deliberately contrived by the poet. Words with two or more meanings may not only give rise to misunderstandings; they may even create confusion in our thoughts. Proust once drew attention to the effects which the ambiguity of the French adjective *grand* may

Here I want to interject the semantic point that such words as life, purpose, and soul are grossly inadequate to precise scientific thinking. These terms have gained their significance through our recognition of the unity of a certain group of phenomena, and do not in fact furnish us with any adequate basis to characterize this unity. Whenever we find a new phenomenon which partakes to some degree of the nature of those which we have already termed "living phenomena," but does not conform to all the associated aspects which define the term "life," we are faced with the problem whether to enlarge the word "life" so as to include them, or to define it in a more restrictive way so as to exclude them. We have encountered this problem in the past in considering viruses, which show some of the tendencies of life—to persist, to multiply, and to organize—but do not express these tendencies in a fully-developed form. Now that certain analogies of behavior are being observed between the machine and the living organism, the problem as to whether the machine is alive or not is, for our purposes, semantic and we are at liberty to answer it one way or the other as best suits our convenience. As Humpty Dumpty says about some of his more remarkable words, "I pay them extra, and make them do what I want."

Norbert Wiener,

*The Human Use of Human Beings: Cybernetics and Society**

The study of language is not new, but only in the present century have scholars directed considerable attention to the ways in which a particular language influences the world-view of its speakers. In a seminal 1929 essay Edward Sapir wrote as follows: "Language is a guide to 'social reality.' Though language is not ordinarily thought of as of essential interest to the students of social science, it powerfully conditions all our thinking about social problems and processes. Human beings do not live in the objective world alone, nor alone in the world of social activity as ordinarily understood, but are very much at the mercy of the particular language which has become the medium of expression for their society. It is quite an illusion to imagine that one adjusts to reality essentially without the use of language and that language is merely an incidental means of solving specific problems of communication or reflection. The fact of the matter is that the 'real world' is to a large extent unconsciously built up on the language habits of the group. No two languages are ever sufficiently similar to be considered as representing the same social reality. The worlds in which different societies live are distinct worlds, not merely the same world with different labels attached." This possibility became a life-long interest of Sapir's Yale student, Benjamin Whorf. The following essay is Whorf's best-known exposition of what has come to be known among linguists and anthropologists as the Sapir-Whorf hypothesis.

"Science and Linguistics" has three major sections. The first, paragraphs 1-3, expresses a view of language Whorf terms "natural logic." According to natural logic, thought precedes language and language is merely the means of communicating thought. The following section, paragraphs 4-14, considers the essential defect of this view. According to Whorf "natural logic" fails to see that the ways in which a given language determines reality will be "background phenomena" which the speakers of that language will not notice. In a language which does not distinguish time and space, for example, speakers will not easily conceive of time and space as separable, so that it will not occur to them that their consideration of time and space as a single concept is linguistically determined, not simply the "natural" way of looking at time and space. Similarly, it is difficult for speakers of English even to conceive of time and space as a single concept, despite the fact that from the viewpoint of modern physics it may be the more efficient way of looking at the physical universe. In his concluding section, paragraph 15 onward, Whorf considers some examples of the different ways in which various languages conceive and classify reality. The discussion of the Hopi Indian language is continued in greater detail elsewhere in this reader in Whorf's "An American Indian Model of the Universe."

Science and Linguistics

Benjamin Whorf

Every normal person in the world, past infancy in years, can and does talk. By virtue of that fact, every person—civilized or uncivilized —carries through life certain naïve but deeply rooted ideas about talking and its relation to thinking. Because of their firm connection with speech habits that have become unconscious and automatic, these notions tend to be rather intolerant of opposition. They are by no means entirely personal and haphazard; their basis is definitely systematic, so that we are justified in calling them a system of natural logic—a term that seems to me preferable to the term common sense, often used for the same thing.

2. According to natural logic, the fact that every person has talked fluently since infancy makes every man his own authority on the process by which he formulates and communicates. He has merely to consult a common substratum of logic or reason which he and everyone else are supposed to possess. Natural logic says that talking is merely an incidental process concerned strictly with communication, not with formulation of ideas. Talking, or the use of language, is supposed only to "express" what is essentially already formulated non-linguistically. Formulation is an independent process, called thought or thinking, and is supposed to be largely indifferent to the nature of

particular languages. Languages have grammars, which are assumed to be merely norms of conventional and social correctness, but the use of language is supposed to be guided not so much by them as by correct, rational, or intelligent THINKING.

3. Thought, in this view, does not depend on grammar but on laws of logic or reason which are supposed to be the same for all observers of the universe—to represent a rationale in the universe that can be "found" independently by all intelligent observers, whether they

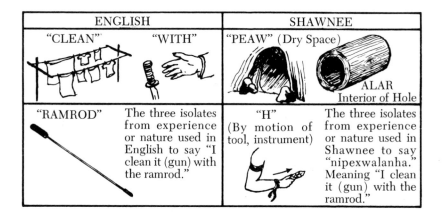

Figure 1. *Languages dissect nature differently. The different isolates of meaning (thoughts) used by English and Shawnee in reporting the same experience, that of cleaning a gun by running the ramrod through it. The pronouns 'I' and 'it' are not shown by symbols, as they have the same meaning in each language. In Shawnee ni- equals 'I'; -a equals 'it.'*

speak Chinese or Choctaw. In our own culture, the formulations of mathematics and of formal logic have acquired the reputation of dealing with this order of things: i.e., with the realm and laws of pure thought. Natural logic holds that different languages are essentially parallel methods for expressing this one-and-the-same rationale of thought and, hence, differ really in but minor ways which may seem important only because they are seen at close range. It holds that mathematics, symbolic logic, philosophy, and so on are systems contrasted with language which deal directly with this realm of thought, not that they are themselves specialized extensions of language. The attitude of natural logic is well shown in an old quip about a German grammarian who devoted his whole life to the study of the dative case. From the point of view of natural logic, the dative case and grammar in general are an extremely minor issue. A different attitude is said to have been held by the ancient Arabians: Two princes, so the story goes, quarreled over the honor of putting on the shoes of the most learned grammarian of the realm; whereupon their father, the caliph, is said to have remarked that it was the glory of his kingdom that great grammarians were honored even above kings.

4. The familiar saying that the exception proves the rule contains a good deal of wisdom, though from the standpoint of formal logic it became an absurdity as soon as "prove" no longer meant "put on trial." The old saw began to be profound psychology from the time it ceased to have standing in logic. What it might well suggest to us today is that, if a rule has absolutely no exceptions, it is not recognized as a rule or as anything else; it is then part of the background of experience of which we tend to remain unconscious. Never having experienced anything in contrast to it, we cannot isolate it and formulate it as a rule until we so enlarge our experience and expand our base of reference that we encounter an interruption of its regularity. The situation is somewhat analogous to that of not missing the water till the well runs dry, or not realizing that we need air till we are choking.

5. For instance, if a race of people had the physiological defect of being able to see only the color blue, they would hardly be able to formulate the rule that they saw only blue. The term blue would convey no meaning to them, their language would lack color terms, and their words denoting their various sensations of blue would answer to, and translate, our words "light, dark, white, black," and so on, not our word "blue." In order to formulate the rule or norm of seeing only blue, they would need exceptional moments in which they saw other colors. The phenomenon of gravitation forms a rule without exceptions; needless to say, the untutored person is utterly unaware of any law of gravitation, for it would never enter his head to conceive of a universe in which bodies behaved otherwise than they do at the earth's surface. Like the color blue with our hypothetical race, the law of gravitation is a part of the untutored individual's background, not something he isolates from that background. The law could not be formulated until bodies that always fell were seen

in terms of a wider astronomical world in which bodies moved in
orbits or went this way and that.

6. Similarly, whenever we turn our heads, the image of the scene
passes across our retinas exactly as it would if the scene turned around
us. But this effect is background, and we do not recognize it; we do
not see a room turn around us but are conscious only of having turned
our heads in a stationary room. If we observe critically while turning
the head or eyes quickly, we shall see, no motion it is true, yet a

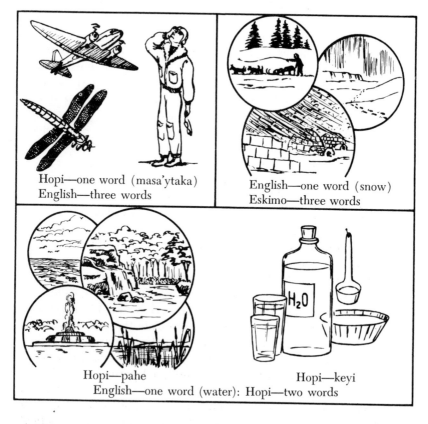

Hopi—one word (masa'ytaka)
English—three words

English—one word (snow)
Eskimo—three words

Hopi—pahe
English—one word (water): Hopi—two words

Hopi—keyi

Figure 2. *Languages classify items of experience differently. The
class corresponding to one word and one thought in language A may
be regarded by language B as two or more classes corresponding to
two or more words and thoughts.*

blurring of the scene between two clear views. Normally we are quite unconscious of this continual blurring but seem to be looking about in an unblurred world. Whenever we walk past a tree or house, its image on the retina changes just as if the tree or house were turning on an axis; yet we do not see trees or houses turn as we travel about at ordinary speeds. Sometimes ill-fitting glasses will reveal queer movements in the scene as we look about, but normally we do not see the relative motion of the environment when we move; our psychic make-up is somehow adjusted to disregard whole realms of phenomena that are so all-pervasive as to be irrelevant to our daily lives and needs.

7. Natural logic contains two fallacies: First, it does not see that the phenomena of a language are to its own speakers largely of a background character and so are outside the critical consciousness and control of the speaker who is expounding natural logic. Hence, when anyone, as a natural logician, is talking about reason, logic, and the laws of correct thinking, he is apt to be simply marching in step with purely grammatical facts that have somewhat of a background character in his own language or family of languages but are by no means universal in all languages and in no sense a common substratum of reason. Second, natural logic confuses agreement about subject matter, attained through use of language, with knowledge of the linguistic process by which agreement is attained: i.e., with the province of the despised (and to its notion superfluous) grammarian. Two fluent speakers, of English let us say, quickly reach a point of assent about the subject matter of their speech; they agree about what their language refers to. One of them, A, can give directions that will be carried out by the other, B, to A's complete satisfaction. Because they thus understand each other so perfectly, A and B, as natural logicians, suppose they must of course know how it is all done. They think, e.g., that it is simply a matter of choosing words to express thoughts. If you ask A to explain how he got B's agreement so readily, he will simply repeat to you, with more or less elaboration or abbreviation, what he said to B. He has no notion of the process involved. The amazingly complex system of linguistic patterns and classifications, which A and B must have in common before they can adjust to each other at all, is all background to A and B.

8. These background phenomena are the province of the grammarian —or of the linguist, to give him his more modern name as a scientist. The word linguist in common, and especially newspaper, parlance

means something entirely different, namely, a person who can quickly attain agreement about subject matter with different people speaking a number of different languages. Such a person is better termed a polyglot or a multilingual. Scientific linguists have long understood that ability to speak a language fluently does not necessarily confer a linguistic knowledge of it, i.e., understanding of its background phenomena and its systematic processes and structure, any more than ability to play a good game of billiards confers or requires any knowledge of the laws of mechanics that operate upon the billiard table.

9. The situation here is not unlike that in any other field of science. All real scientists have their eyes primarily on background phenomena that cut very little ice, as such, in our daily lives; and yet their studies have a way of bringing out a close relation between these unsuspected realms of fact and such decidedly foreground activities as transporting goods, preparing food, treating the sick, or growing potatoes, which in time may become very much modified, simply because of pure scientific investigation in no way concerned with these brute matters themselves. Linguistics presents a quite similar case; the background phenomena with which it deals are involved in all our foreground activities of talking and of reaching agreement, in all reasoning and arguing of cases, in all law, arbitration, conciliation, contracts, treaties, public opinion, weighing of scientific theories, formulation of scientific results. Whenever agreement or assent is arrived at in human affairs, and whether or not mathematics or other specialized symbolisms are made part of the procedure, THIS AGREEMENT IS REACHED BY LINGUISTIC PROCESSES, OR ELSE IT IS NOT REACHED.

10. As we have seen, an overt knowledge of the linguistic processes by which agreement is attained is not necessary to reaching some sort of agreement, but it is certainly no bar thereto; the more complicated and difficult the matter, the more such knowledge is a distinct aid, till the point may be reached—I suspect the modern world has about arrived at it—when the knowledge becomes not only an aid but a necessity. The situation may be likened to that of navigation. Every boat that sails is in the lap of planetary forces; yet a boy can pilot his small craft around a harbor without benefit of geography, astronomy, mathematics, or international politics. To the captain of an ocean liner, however, some knowledge of all these subjects is essential.

11. When linguists became able to examine critically and scientifically a large number of languages of widely different patterns, their base of reference was expanded; they experienced an interruption of phenomena hitherto held universal, and a whole new order of significances came into their ken. It was found that the background linguistic system (in other words, the grammar) of each language is not merely a reproducing instrument for voicing ideas but rather is itself the shaper of ideas, the program and guide for the individual's mental activity, for his analysis of impressions, for his synthesis of his mental stock in trade. Formulation of ideas is not an independent process, strictly rational in the old sense, but is part of a particular grammar, and differs, from slightly to greatly, between different grammars. We dissect nature along lines laid down by our native languages. The categories and types that we isolate from the world of phenomena we do not find there because they stare every observer in the face; on the contrary, the world is presented in a kaleidoscopic flux of impressions which has to be organized by our minds—and this means largely by the linguistic systems in our minds. We cut nature up, organize it into concepts, and ascribe significances as we do, largely because we are parties to an agreement to organize it in this way—an agreement that holds throughout our speech community and is codified in the patterns of our language. The agreement is, of course, an implicit and unstated one, BUT ITS TERMS ARE ABSOLUTELY OBLIGATORY: we cannot talk at all except by subscribing to the organization and classification of data which the agreement decrees.

12. This fact is very significant for modern science, for it means that no individual is free to describe nature with absolute impartiality but is constrained to certain modes of interpretation even while he thinks himself most free. The person most nearly free in such respects would be a linguist familiar with very many widely different linguistic systems. As yet no linguist is in any such position. We are thus introduced to a new principle of relativity, which holds that all observers are not led by the same physical evidence to the same picture of the universe, unless their linguistic backgrounds are similar, or can in some way be calibrated.

13. This rather startling conclusion is not so apparent if we compare only our modern European languages, with perhaps Latin and Greek thrown in for good measure. Among these tongues there is a unanimity of major pattern which at first seems to bear out natural logic. But this unanimity exists only because these tongues are all Indo-European dialects cut to the same basic plan, being historically transmit-

Objective Field	Speaker (Sender)	Hearer (Receiver)	Handling of Topic Running of Third Person
Situation 1a.			English . . . "He is running."
			Hopi . . . "Wari," (running, statement of fact)
Situation 1b.			English . . . "He ran."
Objective field blank devoid of running			Hopi . . . "Wari," (running, statement of fact)
Situation 2.			English . . . "He is running."
			Hopi . . . "Wari," (running, statement of fact)
Situation 3.			English . . . "He ran."
Objective field blank			Hopi . . . "Era wari," (running, statement of fact from memory)
Situation 4.			English . . . "He will run."
Objective field blank			Hopi . . . "Warikni," (running, statement of expectation)
Situation 5.			English . . . "He runs," (e.g. on the track team.)
Objective field blank			Hopi . . . "Warikngwe," (running, statement of law.)

Figure 3. *Contrast between a "temporal" language (English) and a "timeless" language (Hopi). What are to English differences of time are to Hopi differences in the kind of validity.*

ted from what was long ago one speech community; because the modern dialects have long shared in building up a common culture; and because much of this culture, on the more intellectual side, is derived from the linguistic backgrounds of Latin and Greek. Thus this group of languages satisfies the special case of the clause beginning "unless" in the statement of the linguistic relativity principle at the end of the preceding paragraph. From this condition follows the unanimity of description of the world in the community of modern scientists. But it must be emphasized that "all modern Indo-European-speaking observers" is not the same thing as "all observers." That modern Chinese or Turkish scientists describe the world in the same terms as Western scientists means, of course, only that they have taken over bodily the entire Western system of rationalizations, not that they have corroborated that system from their native posts of observation.

14. When Semitic, Chinese, Tibetan, or African languages are contrasted with our own, the divergence in analysis of the world becomes more apparent; and, when we bring in the native languages of the Americas, where speech communities for many millenniums have gone their ways independently of each other and of the Old World, the fact that languages dissect nature in many different ways becomes patent. The relativity of all conceptual systems, ours included, and their dependence upon language stand revealed. That American Indians speaking only their native tongues are never called upon to act as scientific observers is in no wise to the point. To exclude the evidence which their languages offer as to what the human mind can do is like expecting botanists to study nothing but food plants and hothouse roses and then tell us what the plant world is like!

15. Let us consider a few examples. In English we divide most of our words into two classes, which have different grammatical and logical properties. Class 1 we call nouns, e.g., 'house, man'; class 2, verbs, e.g., 'hit, run.' Many words of one class can act secondarily as of the other class, e.g., 'a hit, a run,' or 'to man (the boat),' but, on the primary level, the division between the classes is absolute. Our language thus gives us a bipolar division of nature. But nature herself is not thus polarized. If it be said that 'strike, turn, run,' are verbs because they denote temporary or short-lasting events, i.e., actions, why then is 'fist' a noun? It also is a temporary event. Why are 'lightning, spark, wave, eddy, pulsation, flame, storm, phase, cycle, spasm, noise, emotion' nouns? They are temporary events. If 'man' and 'house' are nouns because they are long-lasting and stable events, i.e., things, what then are 'keep, adhere, extend, project, continue, persist, grow, dwell,' and so on doing among the verbs? If it be objected that 'possess, adhere' are verbs because they are stable relationships rather than stable precepts, why then should 'equilibrium, pressure, current, peace, group, nation, society, tribe, sister,' or any kinship term be among the nouns? It will be found that an "event" to us means "what our language classes as a verb" or something analogized therefrom. And it will be found that it is not possible to define 'event, thing, object, relationship,' and so on, from nature, but that to define them always involves a circuitous return to the grammatical categories of the definer's language.

16. In the Hopi language, 'lightning, wave, flame, meteor, puff of smoke, pulsation' are verbs—events of necessarily brief duration cannot be anything but verbs. 'Cloud' and 'storm' are at about the lower limit of duration for nouns. Hopi, you see, actually has a classification of events (or linguistic isolates) by duration type, something strange to our modes of thought. On the other hand, in Nootka, a language of Vancouver Island, all words seem to us to be verbs, but really there are no classes 1 and 2; we have, as it were, a monistic view of nature that gives us only one class of word for all kinds of events. 'A house occurs' or 'it houses' is the way of saying 'house,' exactly like 'a flame occurs' or 'it burns.' These terms seem to us like verbs because they are inflected for durational and temporal nuances, so that the suffixes of the word for house event make it mean long-lasting house, temporary house, future house, house that used to be, what started out to be a house, and so on.

17. Hopi has one noun that covers every thing or being that flies, with the exception of birds, which class is denoted by another noun. The former noun may be said to denote the class *(FC—B)*—flying class minus bird. The Hopi actually call insect, airplane, and aviator all by the same word, and feel no difficulty about it. The situation, of course, decides any possible confusion among very disparate members of a broad linguistic class, such as this class *(FC—B)*. This class seems to us too large and inclusive, but so would our class 'snow' to an Eskimo. We have the same word for falling snow, snow on the ground, snow packed hard like ice, slushy snow, wind-driven flying snow—whatever the situation may be. To an Eskimo, this all-inclusive word would be almost unthinkable; he would say that falling snow, slushy snow, and so on, are sensuously and operationally different, different things to contend with; he uses different words for them and for other kinds of snow. The Aztecs go even farther than we in the opposite direction, with 'cold,' 'ice,' and 'snow' all represented by the same basic word with different terminations; 'ice' is the noun form; 'cold,' the adjectival form; and for 'snow,' "ice mist."

18. What surprises most is to find that various grand generalizations of the Western world, such as time, velocity, and matter, are not essential to the construction of a consistent picture of the universe. The psychic experiences that we class under these headings are, of course, not destroyed; rather, categories derived from other kinds of experiences take over the rulership of the cosmology and seem to function just as well. Hopi may be called a timeless language. It recognizes psychological time, which is much like Bergson's "duration," but this "time" is quite unlike the mathematical time, T, used by our physicists. Among the peculiar properties of Hopi time are that it varies with each observer, does not permit of simultaneity, and has zero dimensions; i.e., it cannot be given a number greater than one. The Hopi do not say, "I stayed five days," but "I left on the fifth day." A word referring to this kind of time, like the word day, can have no plural. The puzzle picture (Fig. 3) will give mental exercise to anyone who would like to figure out how the Hopi verb gets along without tenses. Actually, the only practical use of our tenses, in one-verb sentences, is to distinguish among five typical situations, which are symbolized in the picture. The timeless Hopi verb does not distinguish between the present, past, and future of the event itself but must always indicate what type of validity the SPEAKER intends the statement to have: (a) report on an event (situations 1, 2, 3 in the picture); (b) expectation of an event (situation 4); (c) generalization or law about events (situation 5). Situation 1, where the speaker and listener are in contact with the same objective field, is divided by our language into the two conditions, 1*a* and 1*b*, which it calls present and past, respectively. This division is unnecessary for a language which assures one that the statement is a report.

19. Hopi grammar, by means of its forms called aspects and modes, also makes it easy to distinguish among momentary, continued, and repeated occurrences, and to indicate the actual sequence of reported events. Thus the universe can be described without recourse to a concept of dimensional time. How would a physics constructed along

these lines work, with no T (time) in its equations? Perfectly, as far as I can see, though of course it would require different ideology and perhaps different mathematics. Of course V (velocity) would have to go too. The Hopi language has no word really equivalent to our 'speed' or 'rapid.' What translates these terms is usually a word meaning intense or very, accompanying any verb of motion. Here is a clue to the nature of our new physics. We may have to introduce a new term I, intensity. Every thing and event will have an I, whether we regard the thing or event as moving or as just enduring or being. Perhaps the I of an electric charge will turn out to be its voltage, or potential. We shall use clocks to measure some intensities, or rather, some RELATIVE intensities, for the absolute intensity of anything will be meaningless. Our old friend acceleration will still be there but doubtless under a new name. We shall perhaps call it V, meaning not velocity but variation. Perhaps all growths and accumulations will be regarded as V's. We should not have the concept of rate in the temporal sense, since, like velocity, rate introduces a mathematical and linguistic time. Of course we know that all measurements are ratios, but the measurements of intensities made by comparison with the standard intensity of a clock or a planet we do not treat as ratios, any more than we so treat a distance made by comparison with a yardstick.

20. A scientist from another culture that used time and velocity would have great difficulty in getting us to understand these concepts. We should talk about the intensity of a chemical reaction; he would speak of its velocity or its rate, which words we should at first think were simply words for intensity in his language. Likewise, he at first would think that intensity was simply our own word for velocity. At first we should agree, later we should begin to disagree, and it might dawn upon both sides that different systems of rationalization were being used. He would find it very hard to make us understand what he really meant by velocity of a chemical reaction. We should have no words that would fit. He would try to explain it by likening it to a running horse, to the difference between a good horse and a lazy horse. We should try to show him, with a superior laugh, that his analogy also was a matter of different intensities, aside from which there was little similarity between a horse and a chemical reaction in a beaker. We should point out that a running horse is moving relative to the ground, whereas the material in the beaker is at rest.

21. One significant contribution to science from the linguistic point of view may be the greater development of our sense of perspective. We shall no longer be able to see a few recent dialects of the Indo-European family, and the rationalizing techniques elaborated from their patterns, as the apex of the evolution of the human mind, nor their present wide spread as due to any survival from fitness or to anything but a few events of history—events that could be called fortunate only from the parochial point of view of the favored parties. They, and our own thought processes with them, can on longer be envisioned as spanning the gamut of reason and knowledge but only as one constellation in galactic expanse. A fair realization of the incredible degree of diversity of linguistic system that ranges over the globe leaves one with an inescapable feeling that the human spirit is inconceivably old; that the few thousand years of history covered by our written records are no more than the thickness of a pencil mark on the scale that measures our past experience on this planet; that the events of these recent millenniums spell nothing in any evolutionary wise, that the race has taken no sudden spurt, achieved no commanding synthesis during recent millenniums, but has only played a little with a few of the linguistic formulations and views of nature bequeathed from an inexpressibly longer past. Yet neither this feeling nor the sense of precarious dependence of all we know upon linguistic tools which themselves are largely unknown need be discouraging to science but should, rather, foster that humility which accompanies the true scientific spirit, and thus forbid that arrogance of the mind which hinders real scientific curiosity and detachment.

If we look closely at our behavior, we say that we view the world in terms of time and space; that, in a way, we place a time grid and a space grid over our experience of the world. We see that others do this as well, and we then generalize and say that this is common to all men—all men see objects in three dimensional space, and the changing relationships of these objects give rise to events which occur along a continuum of time.

The modern physicist, however, is more inclined to say that there is a continuum not only of time but of space *and* time, with the result that we cannot plot objects and events in one grid without plotting them in the other, and, furthermore, it is more efficient to have one four dimensional grid than two separate grids, thereby negating in a sense the distinction between space and time which we normally feel to be both necessary and significant. We explain this relatively easily, though, by noting that the physicist is dealing with very unusual phenomena, namely with objects travelling almost at the speed of light, and since we realize that he has constructed his space-time continuum as a tool to deal with these unusual events, just as he has constructed mathematics, our version of ordinary reality is not threatened. In a way, this is like saying that since the hammer is a manufactured extension of the fist, it is not real or authentic in quite the same way that the fist is real or authentic—it is not to be confused with a real part of the human body.

At this point Whorf enters and reports that he has found people who do not use the grids of time and space, or at least not at all like we do. Probably because of our earlier generalization—that space and time are common to all men—we tend to think that he has discovered people who have hammers where we have fists and find it difficult to see how this can possibly be true unless they are not in fact really human beings. The physicist, for his special purposes, merely modified our ordinary concepts, it seems to us, while Whorf's Hopis have managed without our valuable concepts altogether. Furthermore, we cannot conceive of how reality can be determined without these concepts. What must be seen, it seems to me, is that we, the Hopi, and the physicist are all in the same boat. We are all confronted with sense-data—and you should notice that I cannot avoid using "our" language—and it is up to us to come to terms with it somehow—arrange it, structure it so that our behavior can be directed toward desired ends.

It is roughly at this point that Whorf says that "language determines reality," and we are inclined to say, "Yes, but isn't there a reality beneath language that we could dig down and uncover if only we had the proper tools?" And we tend to conceive of that reality as being the mainspring of the sense-data with which we are confronted, the essences behind our structure. At the same time, we divide this sense-data up, once we are linguistically capable of doing so, into "real," like tables, and chairs in our normal waking state, and "unreal," like things in dreams, mirages, or optical illusions. Part of the problem resides in the fact that "reality" in our language or grammar, functions as a noun or thing. The logic of our language seems to indicate that we can discover reality like we can discover fossils or viruses. If we look at how we determine reality, however, we see that we define things as "real" more on the basis of operational definitions—if you do such and such, and such and such is the result, then you are dealing with something that is real. Reality, then, is more like a value we assign to things in order that our future behavior may be guided to desired results. Any god that is prayed to is real for the person who is praying, and the praying is undertaken with some future state of affairs in mind. We accept some gods as real and reject others because we believe there is a connection between what we desire for the future and the gods we believe in, but no such connection between the future and those we do not believe in. The problem of reality, then, is the problem of what is effective, and it would seem at this point that reality is determined by forms of behavior. At the same time, language is a form of behavior, and in fact it is the only one which enables us to manipulate future events—that is, it seems to me that without language we could not decide that we were going to the bank tomorrow. We may not in fact go to the bank tomorrow, but it is the case that we often do just what we plan to do, and so do the Hopis for that matter. An interesting footnote is that the physical sciences, which in our culture function as a paradigm of truth-seeking, proceed almost completely by operational definitions.

Joe Fitschen, "Footnote to the Problem of Language and Reality" (a student paper)

Susanne Langer, a well-known philosopher, has long been interested in the nature of language. Here she considers the origins of speech and finds it likely that words evolved through a simplification of more elaborate kinds of utterance.

An interesting and controversial aspect of Miss Langer's essay is her distinction between animal and human languages. She suggests five necessary conditions for speech:

(1) the power of elaborate vocalization,
(2) the ability to discriminate heard patterns of sound,
(3) a nervous mechanism that can control speech by distinguishing inner and outer sounds,
(4) the habit of vocal play in groups, and
(5) high mental activity resulting in visual image-making.

Miss Langer suggests that only humans have the last capacity, so that no other animal can use speech. "Animal language is not language at all," she writes, "and what is more important, IT NEVER LEADS TO LANGUAGE." Her argument partially depends on a distinction between expressive and denotative utterance which may be re-examined in the light of conclusions drawn by scientists who have studied the languages of porpoises and bees. Excerpts from important studies of animal language follow Miss Langer's essay.

Speculations on the Origins of Speech and its Communicative Function

Susanne Langer

Ever since the Darwinian theory of human evolution—tracing the descent of man from animal ancestors—has become generally ac-

Reprinted from *Philosophical Sketches* by Susanne Langer, copyright 1962. Reprinted by permission of The Johns Hopkins Press, Baltimore, Maryland.

cepted, the origin of speech has become more and more mystifying. Language is so much the mark of man that it was classically supposed to have been bestowed on him at his creation. But if he has not been created separately from the animals, but has arisen, as most of us now believe, just as they arose, from a more primitive animal ancestry, then surely at some time his own precursors did not speak. When, why, and how did man begin to speak? What generations invented that great social instrument, language? What development of animal communication has eventuated in human communication? What pre-Adamite thought of assigning a particular little squeak to a particular object as the name of that object, by which you could refer to it, demand it, make other people think of it? How did the other pre-Adamites all agree to assign the same squeaks to the same things? What has led to the concatenation of those primitive words in syntactically structured sentences of interrelated meanings? As far as anthropologists know, there is no human language that is not discursive—propositional—in form. Its propositions may be very different from ours, but their semantic structure is always equivalent to what we call a statement. Language always expresses relations among acts or things, or their aspects. It always makes reference to reality—that is, makes assertions or denials—either explicitly or implicitly. Some nouns imply relations, and where they do, verbs may not be needed. In classical Latin the verb is often understood through the inflections of nouns and adjectives. Verbs, in some languages, may imply their subject or object or even both, and make nouns all but unnecessary, as Whorf found in Hopi. But no language consists of signs that only call attention to things without saying anything about them—that is, without asserting or denying something. All languages we know have a fairly stabile vocabulary and a grammatical structure. No language is essentially exclamatory (like ah! and oh!), or emotional (like whining and yodeling), or even imperative. The normal mode of communicative speech, in every human society, is the indicative; and there is no empirical evidence, such as a correlation of increasing discursiveness with increasing culture, to support the belief that it was ever otherwise.

2. Language may be used to announce one's presence, to greet people, to warn, to threaten, to express pain or joy, or even for directing action. Whenever people speak of "animal language" they refer to such uses of observable signs among animals. Leaving aside, for the mo-

ment, the alleged "language" of social insects, we may use the term *vocal signs* among animals.

3. Now, it is an obvious common-sense assumption that human language has grown from some such lower form of vocal communication. But common sense is a very tricky instrument; it is as deceptive as it is indispensable. Because we use it, and have to use it, all the time, we tend to trust it beyond its real credentials, and to feel disconcerted if its simple interpretations of experience fail. Yet common-sense conceptions of the nature and origin of human speech have always led into dilemmas, until the problem of its beginning and development has been generally given up.

4. Even methodology develops its common-sense principles. One of these is that, if you would find the important relationships between two phenomena, you should begin by checking what the phenomena have in common. So, in comparing the vocal communications of animals and men, respectively, we find that all the things animals communicate by sound may also be communicated by human language; and it seems reasonable enough that those things which human language can do and animal vocalization cannot have been added to the primitive animal language, to make the greatly elaborated system of verbal intercourse. But the finding of these common elements leads no further. Common-sense methodology, like the common-sense assumptions, produces nothing more than what we already knew—by common sense.

5. So it may be in order to question our obvious premises, and even depart from the method of seeking common factors in animal and human communication. Instead of noting points of similarity, let us consider the cardinal difference between human and animal language. That difference is in the *uses* to which utterances are put. All those functions that animal and human utterances share—calling, warning, threatening, expressing emotion—are essential uses of animal sounds, and incidental uses of human speech. The functions of animal vocalization are self-expression and sometimes, perhaps, indication of environmental conditions (like the bark of a dog who wants to be let in). The chief function of speech is denotation.

6. Animal language is not language at all, and, what is more important, *it never leads to language*. Dogs that live with men learn to understand many verbal signals, but only as signals, in relation to their own actions. Apes that live in droves and seem to communicate fairly well never *converse*. But a baby that has only half a dozen words begins to converse: "Daddy gone." "Daddy come? Daddy come." Question and answer, assertion and denial, denotation and description—these are the basic uses of language.

7. The line between animal and human estate is, I think, the language line; and the gap it marks between those two kinds of life is almost as profound as the gap between plants and animals. This makes it plausible that we are not dealing with just a higher form of some general animal function, but with a new function developed in the hominid brain—a function of such complexity that probably not one, but many, subhuman mental activities underlie it.

8. The complexity of living forms and functions is something that we are apt to underestimate in speculating on the origins of psychological phenomena. In textbook accounts the facts have to be generalized and simplified to make them comprehensible to beginners; but as soon as you tackle the monographic literature presenting actual cases of growth, maturation, and the conduct of life, and follow actual analyses of function and structure, especially in neurology, the complexity and variability of vital processes are brought home to you with great force. Consider only the chemical activities, that differ enough from any one organism to another to produce the so-called "individuality factor." Or think of the structural organization of the brain; in the small brain center known as the "lateral geniculate body" where the optic nerve ceases to be one bundle of fibers and fans out toward the cortex of the occipital lobe, anatomists have found scores of so-called "boutons," points of reception or emission of electrical impulses, directly on nerve cells, besides the synaptic connections of the branching axons and dendrites of those cells. The potentialities of such a brain for different courses of activity run into billions and trillions, so that even if inhibiting mechanisms eliminate a hundred thousand connections at a time, the range of possible responses, especially in the crowded circuits of the forebrain, is as good as infinite.

9. It is very wholesome for a philosopher who tries to conceive of what we call "mind" to take a long look at neurological exhibits, because in psychological studies we usually see and consider only the integrated products—actions and intentions and thoughts—and with regard to speech, words and their uses. Words seem to be the elements of speech; they are the units that keep their essential identity in different relational patterns, and can be separately moved around.

They keep their "roots" despite grammatical variations, despite prefixes and suffixes and other modifications. A word is the ultimate semantic element of speech. A large class of our words—most of the nouns, or names—denote objects, and objects are units that can enter into many different situations while keeping their identity, much as words can occur in different statements. This relation gives great support to the conception of words as the units of speech.

10. And so, I think, they are. But this does not mean that they are original elements of speech, primitive units that were progressively combined into propositions. Communication, among people who inherit language, begins with the word—the baby's or foreigner's unelaborated key word, that stands proxy for a true sentence. But that word has a phylogenetic history, the rise of language, in which probably neither it nor any archaic version of it was an element.

11. I think it likely that words have actually emerged through progressive simplification of a much more elaborate earlier kind of utterance, which stemmed, in its turn, from several quite diverse sources, and that none of its major sources were forms of animal communication, though some of them were communal.

12. These are odd-sounding propositions, and I am quite aware of their oddness, but perhaps they are not so fantastic as they sound. They merely depart rather abruptly from our usual background assumptions. For instance, the idea that a relatively simple part of a complex phenomenon might not be one of its primitive factors, but might be a product of progressive simplification, goes against our methodological canons. Ever since Thomas Hobbes set up the so-called genetic method of understanding, we have believed that the simplest concepts into which we could break down our ideas of a complex phenomenon denoted the actual elements of that phenomenon, the factors out of which it was historically compounded. Locke's construction of human experience from pure and simple sense data, Condillac's fancied statue endowed with one form of perception after another, and in our own time Bertrand Russell's "logical atomism," all rest on this belief. But close empirical study of vital processes in nature does not bear it out. A great many advanced behavior patterns *are* elaborations of simpler responses, but some are simplifications of very complicated earlier forms of action. The same holds true of the structures that implement them. When the reflex arc was discovered, physiologists felt themselves in possession of a key to all animal response, for here was a simple unit that could be supposed to engender all higher forms by progressive elaboration. But Herrick and Coghill, through careful studies of salamanders in their larval stages, found that the reflex arc is not a primitive structure ontogenetically at all, but is preceded by much more elaborate arrangements in the embryo that undergo simplifications until a unified afferent-efferent circuit results. This finding was corroborated by Lorente de Nó.

13. A principle that is operative in the development of an individual is at least possible in the larger development of a stock. There is nothing absurd about the hypothesis that the simple units in a very advanced function, such as human speech, may be simplifications within an earlier more intricate vocal pattern.

14. Most theories of the origin of language presuppose that man was already man, with social intentions, when he began to speak. But in fact, man must have been an animal—a high primate, with a tendency to live in droves like most of the great apes—when he began to speak. And it must have been rather different from the ancient progenitors of our apes, which evidently lacked, or at least never possessed in combination, those traits that have eventuated in speech.

15. What were those traits? Speech is such a complex function that it has probably not arisen from any single source. Yet if it developed naturally in the hominid stock, every one of its constituents must have started from some spontaneous animal activity, not been invented for a purpose; for only human beings invent instruments for a purpose preconceived. Before speech there is no conception; there are only perceptions, and a characteristic repertoire of actions, and a readiness to act according to the enticements of the perceived world. In speech as we know it, however, there seems to be one flowing, articulate symbolic act in which conventional signs are strung together in conventional ways without much trouble, and similar processes evoked in other persons, all as nicely timed as a rally of ping-pong. Nothing seems more integral and self-contained than the outpouring of language in conversation. How is one ever to break it down into primitive acts?

16. It was from the psychiatric literature on language—on aphasia, paraphasia, agrammatism, alexia, and kindred subjects—that something like a guiding principle emerged. The most baffling thing about the cerebral disturbances of speech is, what strange losses people can sustain: loss of grammatical form without any loss or confusion of words, so that the patient can speak only in "telegraph style"; or contrariwise, loss or confusion of words without loss of sentence structure, so that speech flows in easy sentencelike utterances, but only the prepositions, connectives, and vocal punctuations are recognizable; the informative words all garbled or senseless. Lewis Carroll's

> 'T was brillig, and the slithy toves
> Did gyre and gimble in the wabe

illustrates this separation of sentence form and verbal content. There may be inability to understand spoken language, but not inability to understand printed or written language, yet without any defect of hearing, or the other way about—inability to read, but not to understand speech—without any ocular trouble. There are cases of alexia for words but not for letters, and the recognition, naming, and using of numbers are often intact where neither letters nor words can be recognized. Furthermore, some brain injuries leave the victim able to repeat words spoken for him, but not to speak spontaneously, and others make him unable to repeat words just heard, but not unable to utter them in spontaneous speech. There are even several cases on record of persons in whom a cerebral lesion caused inability to name any inanimate object, but not inability to name living things, or call people by their proper names, and, conversely, cases of inability to name persons, animals, or any parts of them, but not to find the words for inanimate objects like watches and slippers.

17. In the face of these peculiar, sometimes really bizarre exhibits, it occurred to me that what can be separately lost from the integral phenomenon of speech may have been separately developed in the prehistoric, prehuman brain. Here is at least a working notion of a new way to break down the verbal process that might yield a new conception of what has gone into it.

18. In singling out such elements, and trying to trace them back to some plausible—though of course hypothetical—prehuman proclivities, one meets with the surprising fact that some of these habits, that may be supposed to have prepared speech, actually exist in the animal kingdom, and are even quite highly developed, sometimes in relatively low animals. But they are far from any kind of speech. They are raw, unassembled materials, that would be needed in conjunction, as a foundation, if speech were to arise. In the prehuman primate they must have coincided at some time to provide that foundation.

19. This principle of analysis takes us much further back into pre-paratory phases of mental development than the usual anthropological approach to the problem of speech, which reaches back only to the supposed archaic forms of genuine language. Not only mental activities, but some grosser somatic conditions that made them possible, must have met in the animal stock that produced the human race. For instance, the continuity of language requires a bodily mechanism that can sustain a long process of vocalization. Not all animals can do that; it is interesting that the chimpanzee, which is nearest to man in mental capacity, cannot sustain a vowel sound; also it rarely produces a pure and simple sound. Its larynx is too complicated, and it has more than one source of air supply for it, and no fine control of a single set of bellows to mete out its vocal power. The gibbon has a simpler larynx, more like ours, and also the requisite propensity to utter long, chantlike ululations in chorus: that is, it has the physical powers of vocalization, and the habit of using them in a gathered company—two prerequisites for speech. But its brain is too inferior to endow its joyful noise with anything but self-expression and mutual stimulation to keep it up.

20. Another condition of speech is the epicritical ear, that distin-guishes one sound from another, beyond the usual distinction of noises according to their sources—that is, beyond distinguishing them as calls of other creatures, as footsteps, perhaps as the splash of water, and for the rest either as meaningless rumbles and creaks, or not at all. The epicritical power of hearing requires a highly specialized cochlea and a distribution of the auditory nerve in the brain that is not found in all the higher animals, but occurs in several birds—an anomalous development in a relatively low type of brain. Those birds that imitate the whistles of other birds and the sounds of human speech, whereby we know they have a highly analytic hearing (which anatomical findings bear out), have something more that is relevant to our own powers: the control of the vocal apparatus by the ear, which seems to be rudimentary in most animals, although the mecha-nisms of hearing and sound-making are always associated—even in the cricket, which has its peripheral organs of hearing in the thighs. The kind of feedback that molds an utterance according to sounds heard, and makes formal imitation possible, is another specialization beyond the epicritical receptor organ. Dogs have the fine receptor, the ear that discriminates articulate sounds within a general category, for they can respond selectively to quite a gamut of verbal signals, and Pavlov found their discrimination of tonal pitch superior to man's; but dogs never show the slightest impulse or ability to imitate foreign sounds.

21. So we find several prerequisites for speech—sustained and variable vocalization, the tendency to responsive utterance, the epicritical hearing and fine control of vocalization by the ear that implement imitation—pre-figured in the behavior patterns of widely different animals. Yet none of those animals use language. These traits are only some of its conditions, and even they do not coincide in any one species. In the protohuman primate they must have coincided—not only with each other, but with some further ones as well, that may or may not occur in other creatures.

22. The decisive function in the making of language comes, I think, from quite another quarter than the vocal-auditory complexes that serve its normal expression. That other quarter is the visual system, in which the visual image—the paradigm of what, therefore, we call "imagination"—almost certainly is produced.

23. How a visual image is engendered and what nervous mechanisms participate in its creation no one has yet described; I have gathered a few ideas on the subject, but they need not detain us here. The important thing is that images are the things that naturally take on the character of symbols. Images are "such stuff as dreams are made on"; dreams have the tendency to assume symbolic value, apparently very early in our lives, and the peculiar involutions of meaning in their imagery, the vagueness of connections, the spontaneity of their presentations, and the emotional excitement of any very vivid dream may well reflect the nature of primitive symbolic experience.

24. The old problem, how words became attached to objects as their distinctive names, and how they became generalized so that they denoted kinds of things rather than individuals, may find its solution if we can give up the notion that primitive man *invented* speech, and agreed on names for things and other basic conventions. I do not believe names were originally assigned to things at all; *naming* is a process that presupposes speech. Now that we have language, we can give names to new comets, new gadgets, and constantly to new babies. But in the making of speech, I think it more likely that definite phonetic structures were already at hand, developed in another context, and that meanings accrued to them—vaguely and variably at

first, but by natural processes that tended to specify and fix them. Such meanings were not pragmatic signal values of specific sounds for specific things; several eminent psychiatrists to the contrary notwithstanding, primitive denotation was not like using a proper name. When words took shape, they were general in intent, from the beginning; their connotations inhered in them, and their denotations were whatever fitted this inherent sense.

25. Now that I have thus pontificated on what happened, let me explain why I think something like this must have happened, and how it would account for the greatest of all mysteries of language—the fact that language is symbolic, when no animal utterance shows any tendency that way. The biological factors that caused this great shift in the vocal function were, I believe, the development of visual imagery in the humanoid brain, and the part it came to play in a highly exciting, elating experience, the festal dance. (How prehuman beings advanced from animal behavior to formalized tribal dance is another relevant subject I cannot broach here.) The mental image was, I think, the catalyst that precipitated the conceptual import of speech.

26. As I remarked before, images are more prone than anything else we know to become symbols; they have several attributes that work together to make them symbolic. So it was another of the evolutionary coincidences that the Calibans who preceded us suffered a peculiar specialization in their visual systems, so that we produce mental images without even trying—most successfully, in fact, while we sleep.

27. There is a reason, of course, why this should be a hominid specialty, and we can at least guess what caused our odd and rather impractical habit of *visualizing*, with and without stimulation from the end organs, the eyes. The human brain presumably developed, like any animal brain we know, as a mediating organ between afferent impulses and their efferent completion, that is, their spending themselves in action. In animals, typically, every stimulation that takes effect at all is spent in some overt act, which may be anything from a reflex twitch of the skin to a directed act of the whole aroused creature. But the messages which come into our brains are so many and various that it would be impossible and exhausting to spend each afferent impulse in overt action. So a great many, especially the countless visual impressions we take in, have to be finished within the brain; the cerebral response is the formation of an image. This automatic process may occur in animals, too, but sporadically and at a lower intensity, and therefore without further consequences. If animals have images, I don't think they are bothered by them or use them; such passing visions may be like our after-images, automatic products of sensory stimulation.

28. In human beings, however, image making has become a normal conclusion for acts of focused gazing. Since, in the waking state, it is easier to look at things than not to, image production is generally effortless and unintentional, and in the normal course of development soon becomes so rich that there is a constant play of imagery. Every impression is apt to produce an image, however briefly and incompletely, and out of this welter a few more definite visualizations emerge at intervals.

29. The several characteristics that make the mental image prone to become symbolic are, in the first place, this spontaneous, quasi-automatic production; secondly, a tendency of image-making processes to mesh, and pool their results; then, their origin in actual perception which gives images an obvious relation to the sources of perception—things perceived—a relation we call "representation"; furthermore, the very important fact that an image, once formed, can be reactivated in many ways, by all sorts of external and internal stimulations; and finally, its involvement with emotion. Let us consider what each of these traits has to do with the making of the primitive symbol, and with the enlistment of the vocal organs for its projection.

30. A biological mechanism that is about to assume a new function is usually developed at least somewhat beyond the needs of its original function—that is, its activity has a certain amount of play, sometimes called "excess energy," which allows unpredictable developments. A new departure is not likely to be based on rare occurrences, for to become established it has to survive many miscarriages, and that means that it has to begin over and over again—that is, the conditions for it have to be generous. So, in a brain where imagination was to take on a new and momentous function—symbolization—the production of images had to be a vigorous business, generating images all the time, so that most of them could be wasted, and the symbolic activity could still begin again and again, and proceed to various degrees, without interfering with the normal functions of the brain in the whole organic economy. So the normality and ease of image producing met one of the first requisites for the rise of a higher function.

31. The second important feature of mental images for symbol making is the fact that the processes of imagination seem particularly prone to affect each other, to mingle and mesh and share their paths of activity, inhibiting or reinforcing nervous impulses in progress, and especially inducing all sorts of neighboring reactions. Consequently their products tend to fuse: images that share some features fuse into one image with emphasis on those features, which thereby are stressed, and dominate the welter of other characters that, for their part, are weakened by fusion. Images, therefore, modify each other; some dominate others, and all tend to become simplified. Emphasis is what gives contours and gradients and other structural elements to images. Emphasis is the natural process of abstraction, whereby our visual representations are made to differ from the direct perceptions that started them. Rudolph Arnheim in his book, *Art and Visual Perception,* has gone quite deeply into the distinctions between the laws of perception and those of representation. The point of interest here is that the power of abstract symbolic thinking, which plays such a great part in later human mentality, rests on a relatively primitive talent of abstractive seeing that comes with the nature of the visual image.

32. The third major condition is simply the fact that images stem from percepts, and the process of their derivation is an original continuity of a peripheral event, the effect of a visible object on the eye, with the further nervous events that terminate in the formation of an image in the brain. The eye is the end organ of the visual apparatus; what goes on behind the retina, and especially, perhaps, beyond the chiasma, is the rest of our seeing, with all its reverberations and complications and their astounding effects. The recognition of an image as something connected with the external world is intuitive, as the response to external things in direct visual perception, which all seeing animals exhibit, is instinctive. This recognition of images as representations of visible things is the basis on which the whole public importance of symbols is built—their use for reference. But there must have been another coincidence to make that happen.

33. This crucial fourth factor is really part of that lability of imagination, and openness to influence, that we have already remarked; but more precisely, it is the fact that the occurrence of an image may be induced by a great many different kinds of stimulation, either from outside the organism or from within. Often one cannot tell what

evokes a mental image; sometimes a whole situation that often recurs will always do it; for instance, whenever you step out on a pier and smell salt water you may have an image of your first sailboat. Even the salt smell alone may invoke it. So may the mention of the boat's name. Those are more specific stimuli, but there can be all kinds. This readiness to occur in a total context, but also to be touched off by small fragments of that context encountered in other settings, is the trait that frees the mental image from its original connection with peripheral vision, that is, from the thing it first represented. Add to this the tendency of images with traits in common to fuse and make a simplified image—that is, to become schematic—and you see how much of our image making would become casual acts if ideation, without any specific memory bonds to perceptual experiences. Not only the images themselves that share a schematic character, but also their representational functions fuse; and one of them can represent the original percept of any other; that is, as representations whole families of them can stand proxy one for another. Any image of a grasshopper can represent any grasshopper we have actually seen that was not so distinctive that it created an image too different to fit the schema. If such an oddity appears we form an image of a *special kind* of grasshopper. With its liberation from perception the image becomes general; and as soon as it can represent something else than its own original stimulus, it becomes a symbol. Schematic similarities in otherwise distinct images make it possible to recall one object through the image of another. Thus, for instance, the outline of the new moon is like that of a small curved boat. We can see the moon as a canoe, or a canoe as a moon. Either assimilation reinforces the perception of shape. This is the natural process of abstraction. We speak of the sickle, the bowl, the disk of the moon in its various phases. In developed thinking we know whether we are talking about the moon or about a boat—that is, we know which image is standing proxy for the other. But studies in the symbolic functions occurring in dream and myth and some psychoses give support to the belief that this is a sober insight which was probably not very early. At the level of prehuman image mongering, the question is rather how one image, even without sensory support, becomes dominant over others, so that they are its symbolic representatives in imagination.

34. Here, the mechanism seems to be the connection of imagery with emotion. In the complex of images, the one most charged with emotion becomes the dominant image which all the others repeat, reinforce, and represent within the brain itself, even below the level of awareness—in the limbo of what Freud called "the dream work," whereby the significant images, the symbols for conception, are made. 35. These are, I think, the main physical and behavioral factors that must have existed conjointly in the one animal species that has developed speech: the power of elaborate vocalization, the discriminative ear that heard patterns of sounds, the nervous mechanisms that controlled utterance by hearing inner and outer sounds, and the tendency to utter long passages of sound in gatherings of many individuals— that is, the habit of joint ululation—with considerable articulation that recurred at about the same point within every such occasion, and, in these same beings, the high mental activity that issued in visual image making. The gatherings were probably communal rituals, or rather, awesome aesthetic precursors of genuine ritual, the ululations the vocal elements in primitive dance. This idea was propounded long ago by J. Donovan, but no one seems to have paid much attention to it. I adopted it in an early book, *Philosophy in a New Key,* and the more I reflect on it the more I think it is sound. It was Donovan's idea that words were not primitive elements in human utterance when it became symbolic, but that meaning first accrued to longer passages, which were gradually broken or condensed into separate bits, each with its own fixed sense. But what he did not say—and I did not see, twenty years ago—was how conceptual meaning accrued to any vocal products at all. I certainly never realized what part the private mental image played in preparing the way for symbolic language—that the whole mechanism of symbolization was probably worked out in the visual system before its power could be transferred to the vocalauditory realm. Now, with that helpful surmise, let us see how the transfer would be possible, and not too improbable.

36. In the elaborate development of tribal dance all individuals of the primitive horde became familiar with the vocal sounds that belonged to various sequences of steps and gestures, some perhaps mimetic, others simply athletic, but working up to climaxes of excitement. The "song," or vocal part of the dance, became more and more differentiated with the evolution of the gestic patterns. At high points there were undoubtedly special shouts and elaborate halloos. In the overstimulated brains of the celebrants, images must have been evoked at these points of action and special vocalization—images that

tended to recur in that context, until for each individual his own symbolic images were built into the familiar patterns of tribal rituals. A dance passage takes time and energy and usually several persons to produce, but the vocal ingredient can be produced with little effort and a minimum of time by any individual. To remember the dance would bring the vocal element to his throat; as the memory of playing "London Bridge" will usually cause a child to hum the tune,

"Lon-don Bridge is fal-ling down,"

with no thought of a bridge or a fair lady, but of the game. So people could reactivate their emotional symbolic images by a snatch of the festal songs. If the dance action is, say, swinging a club, or even feels like that familiar and expansive act, the various images evoked will be of a club, or clubs, or raising or swinging clubs, or cracking them against each other. It is the image that symbolizes the activity and the objects involved in it. The image is the magical effect of the sound pattern when it is intoned apart from the dance.

37. The image is a pure conception; it does not signalize or demand its object, but denotes it. Of course, this denotative symbol, the image, begets no communication, for it is purely private. But the things imaged are public, and the sounds that activate images are public; they affect everybody by evoking images at roughly the same moments of dance action. Within a fairly wide range it does not matter how different the private images are. They are equivalent symbols for the act or the objects that mark those stations in the ritual where the vocal bits belong, which may be uttered out of context by some individual; and suddenly meaning accrues to the phrase, other beings *understand*, especially if a connoted object is physically at hand, apart from its ritual context.

38. I suspect that the first meanings of such secularized vocalization were very vague; swing a club, hit a man with a club, kill man and beast, whirl and hit, get hit, wave a club at the moon—may all have belonged by turns to one long utterance, in which the separate articulate parts need not have had any separable meanings. But once such passages were used to evoke ideas, their vocalization would quickly become modified, especially by reduction to the *speaking voice*, which can utter its sounds with more speed and less effort than any singing voice. This everyday utterance would tend to emphasize vowels and consonants—that is, mouth articulations—to replace distinctions of

pitch. Some languages today use tonal distinctions, without precise pitch, as semantic devices. But in most human speech, tones serve only for punctuation and emotional coloring.

39. The great step from anthropoid to anthropos, animal to man, was taken when the vocal organs were moved to register the occurrence of an image, and stirred an equivalent occurrence in another brain, and the two creatures referred to the same thing. At that point, the vocal habit that had long served for communion assumed the function of communication. To evoke ideas in each other's minds, not in the course of action, but of emotion and memory—that is, in reflection—is to communicate *about* something, and that is what no animals do.

40. From then on, speech probably advanced with head-long speed; the vaguely articulated phrases of the gathered horde contracted around their cores of meaning and made long, rich, omnibus words, and broke up into more specifically denotative words, until practically the whole phonetic repertoire was formalized into separable bits, and language entered the synthetic stage of making sentences out of words—the reverse of its pristine articulative process. The new motive of communication must have driven it like wildfire. At this stage if not before, the actual evocation of images became dispensable. We do not need vision to learn speech. The symbolic function has passed to the act of speech itself, and from there finally to the word itself, so that even hearing may be prosthetically replaced. For when verbalization is complete, people have not only speech, but language.

41. I think there were other uses of speechlike utterance, too—the principle of tracking down the elements of language that may be separately lost by cerebral impairment even today leads in many directions. Proper names may not have had the same origin as genuine nouns, and numerals are something different again; onomatopoetic words, too, seem to have had their own genesis, apart from the main source of language. But under the influence of language all utterances tended to become words. This is still the case. For instance, our expletives, that have no real verbal meaning in present-day language, always fall under its influence. Only a German says "ach"—most Americans cannot even pronounce it—he says "au" where an American says "ouch;" and who but a Frenchwoman would ever say "ou-la-la"?

42. Once communication got started, the rise of human mentality may have been cataclysmic, a matter of a few generations wherever it

began at all. It must have been an exciting and disconcerting phase
of our history. We have traces of it even to this day in the holy fear
in which many people hold divine names, blessings, curses, magic
formulas—all verbal fragments, imbued with the mystic power of
thought that came with speech.

43. In looking back over all these processes that must have come together to beget language, I am struck by a few outstanding facts:
in the first place, the depth to which the foundations go, on which
this highest of all creature attainments is built; secondly, the complexity of all living functions, for every one of those preparatory traits
was itself a highly integrated complex of many nervous processes; in
the third place, the fact that not one of the constituents in the new
and fateful talent was a mode of animal communication. It seems
most likely that the office of communication was taken over by speech,
from entirely different activities, when speech was well started; but
undoubtedly communication was what henceforth made its history.
Finally, it is a notable fact that the two senses which hold the greatest
places in the human cortex, sight and hearing, were both needed to
produce language; neither a sightless nor a deaf race could have
evolved it. If man could either hear no evil or see no evil, he could
speak no evil—nor yet any good.

> . . . the round dance and the wagging dance are two different
> terms in the language of bees, the former meaning a source of
> food near the hive and the latter a source at 100 meters or more
> . . . the wagging dance not only announces that there is a
> rich source that is far away; it also tells *how* far away. The dis-
> tance is indicated in a rather exact manner by the number of
> turns in the wagging dance that are made in a given time. . . .
> there is a definite rate for any distance which is characteristic of
> a particular colony of bees; that is, the curves relating the rate
> of turning to the distance of the food often vary from one colony
> to another. . . . the rate varies with the direction of the wind.
> A head wind on the way to the feeding place has the same effect
> as increased distance; it slows the dances. A tail wind has the
> opposite effect. . . . The language of bees is truly perfect, and
> their method of indicating the direction of food sources is one
> of the most remarkable mysteries of their complex social or-
> ganization. . . . One cannot believe that bees decided all at
> once to arrange matters thus. We may be sure that this meaning-

ful relationship has developed gradually. . . . It would be of
great interest to investigate more primitive social insects to learn
whether they have a simpler kind of language which would show
us how the complex situation found in honeybees may have been
developed.

Karl von Frisch,

*Bees**

Animals do not possess a language in the true sense of the
word. In the higher vertebrates, as also in insects, . . . every individual has a certain number of innate movements and sounds for
expressing feelings. It has also innate ways of reacting to these
signals whenever it sees or hears them in a fellow-member of
the species. The highly social species of birds . . . have a complicated code of such signals. . . . The perfect co-ordination of social
behaviour . . . brought about by these actions and reactions conveys . . . the impression that the birds are talking and understanding a language of their own. . . . this purely innate signal code of
an animal species differs fundamentally from human language,
every word of which must be learned laboriously by the human
child. . . . being a genetically fixed character of the species . . .
this so-called language is, for every individual animal species,
ubiquitous in its distribution. . . The superficial similarity between these animal utterances and human languages diminishes
further as it becomes . . . clear to the observer that the animal, in
all these sounds and movements expressing its emotions, has in
no way the conscious intention of influencing a fellow-member
of its species. . . . the automatic and even mechanical character
of these signals . . . reveals them as entirely different from human
words. . . . All expressions of animal emotions . . . are not comparable to our spoken language, but only to those expressions such
as yawning, . . . and smiling, which are expressed unconsciously
as innate actions and also understood by a corresponding inborn
mechanism. The "words" of the various animal "languages" are
merely interjections.

Konrad Lorenz,

From *King Solomon's Ring***
(translated by Marjorie Kerr Wilson)

. . . it may be possible for humans to speak with another species. I have come to this conclusion after careful consideration of evidence gained through my research experiments with dolphins. . . . the first thing we should look for in any species with which we may try to communicate is a brain comparable in size and complexity to the human brain. Having found such a species, we should attempt to determine whether its members have an intra-species language. . . . Next we should determine whether individuals of the non-human species can be taught a human language. . . . the animal should be capable of vocalizing within the same ranges and parametric sets of variables that the human uses. . . . it should be capable of making *sounds* with its vocal apparatus . . . which sound like human-produced sounds. . . . The animals that best seem to fulfill all of the above qualifications are the dolphins. . . . [If] . . . a dolphin [is] . . . forced to obtain satisfaction of his needs through vocalizations with and from human beings, then the beginnings of language may . . . be inculcated. . . . we demonstrated quite satisfactorily that a dolphin can vocalize in two different ways . . . under water, and . . . by emitting air through his blow-hole so that he produces air-borne sounds that we can hear. We do not know to what degree these animals communicate with one another, but it looks as if they do so at a very complex descriptive level. . . . It is probable that their intelligence is comparable to ours. . . . To accomplish anything of importance with them, we must overcome our self-immolation, xenophobia, and various taboos . . .

John C. Lilly,

Man and Dolphin

In this brief excerpt from LANGUAGE AND MYTH, Ernst Cassirer discusses the identity of the two. He suggests that the closeness of language and myth derives from their simultaneous evolution in the unconscious. He contends that names "fix" reality (an argument related to Whorf's suggestion that the language we learn limits the concepts we can form). To demonstrate this "word power," he traces the religious and secular associations of "names." The religious use of "word," he postulates, is typified by the many Creation legends in which the Word is seen either as the Creator, or as the Creative Force. In some dualistic religions, the power of the word is seen in the prayers which conquer evil and preserve creation for the good. Still other religions hold that knowing the true name of God gives man power over Him, or that the immortality of the soul depends upon naming God correctly.

The secular awareness of "word power" he discusses is typified by the importance of names, including the unseverable linking of the name with its bearer. Thus, when Cyclops is tricked and blinded by Odysseus, he cries out "No-one has blinded me!" for he cannot separate the man from the name, nor consider the meaning of the name. Since the name is inseparable personal property of its bearer, the possibility of harming a man by "taking his name in vain" also arises. Additional recognition of the importance of names in secular tradition is shown by the Eskimo belief in the tri-partite man composed of body, soul, and name, or the Roman refusal to give proper names to slaves because a slave was not a "legal person." The name is felt to emphasize individuality, so that, in many societies, the name is changed at each important event in a man's life.

Cassirer contends, then, that the religious and secular awareness of the power of the "word" or the "name" is derived from a process of the unconscious which produces both language and mythology (resembling the "image-formation process" discussed by Susanne Langer in her essay). The result of this process is an identification of the "name" with the "thing." Thus, the "word" is the "object" it identifies.

Word Magic: The Primitive Power of Language

Ernst Cassirer

(translated by Susanne Langer)

The original bond between the linguistic consciousness and the mythical-religious consciousness is primarily expressed in the fact that all verbal structures appear *also* as mythical entities endowed with certain mythical powers. The Word, in fact, becomes a sort of primary force, in which all being and doing originate. In all mythical cosmogonies, as far back as they can be traced, this supreme position of the Word is found. Among the texts which Preuss has collected among the Uitoto Indians there is one which he has adduced as a direct parallel to the opening passage of St. John, and which, in his translation, certainly seems to fall in with it perfectly: "In the beginning," it says, "the Word gave the Father his origin." Of course, striking though it may be, no one would try to argue from this coincidence to any direct relationship or even an analogy of material content between that primitive creation story and the speculations of St. John.

And yet it presents us with a certain problem, it points to the fact that some indirect relationship must obtain, which covers everything from the most primitive gropings of mythico-religious thought to those highest products in which such thought seems to have already gone over into a realm of pure speculation.

2. A more precise insight into the foundations of this relationship can be attained only in so far as we are able to carry back the study of those examples of Word veneration, which the history of religions is always uncovering, from the mere analogy of their respective *contents* to the recognition of their common *form*. There must be some particular, essentially unchanging *function* that endows the Word with this extraordinary, religious character, and exalts it *ab initio* to the religious sphere, the sphere of the "holy." In the creation accounts of almost all great cultural religions, the Word appears in league with the highest Lord of creation; either as the tool which he employs or actually as the primary source from which he, like all other Being and order of Being, is derived. Thought and its verbal utterance are usually taken directly as one; for the mind that thinks and the tongue that speaks belong essentially together. Thus, in one of the earliest records of Egyptian theology, this primary force of "the heart and the tongue" is attributed to the creation-god Ptah, whereby he produces and governs all gods and men, all animals, and all that lives. Whatever is has come into being through the thought of his heart and the command of his tongue; to these two, all physical and spiritual being, the existence of the Ka as well as all properties of things, owe their origin. Here, as indeed certain scholars have pointed out, thousands of years before the Christian era, God is conceived as a spiritual Being who *thought* the world before he created it, and who used the *Word* as a means of expression and an instrument of creation. And as all physical and psychical Being rest in him, so do all ethical bonds and the whole moral order.

3. Those religions which base their world picture and their cosmogony essentially on a fundamental ethical contrast, the dualism of good and evil, venerate the spoken Word as the primary force by whose sole agency Chaos was transformed into an ethico-religious Cosmos. According to the Bundahish, the cosmogony and cosmography of the Parsis, the war between the power of Good and the power of Evil, i.e., between Ahura Mazda and Angra Mainyu, begins with Ahura Mazda's reciting the words of the Holy Prayer (Ahuna Vairya):

"He spake that which has twenty-one words. The end, which is his victory, the impotence of Angra Mainyu, the decline of the Daevas, the resurrection and the future life, the ending of opposition to the (good) creation for all eternity—all these he showed to Angra Mainyu . . . When a third of this prayer had been spoken, Angra Mainyu doubled up his body with terror, when two-thirds had been spoken he fell upon his knees, and when the whole had been uttered he was confounded, and powerless to abuse the creatures of Ahura Mazda, and remained confounded for three thousand years."

4. Here, again the words of the prayer precede the material creation, and preserve it ever against the destructive powers of the Evil One. Similarly, in India, we find the power of the Spoken Word (Vāc) exalted even above the might of the gods themselves:

"On the Spoken Word all the gods depend, all beasts and men; in the Word live all creatures . . . the Word is the Imperishable, the first-born of the eternal Law, the mother of the Veddas, the navel of the divine world."

5. As the Word is first in origin, it is also supreme in power. Often it is the *name* of the deity, rather than the god himself, that seems to be the real source of efficacy. Knowledge of the name gives him who knows it mastery even over the being and will of the god. Thus a familiar Egyptian legend tells how Isis, the great sorceress, craftily persuaded the sun-god Ra to disclose his name to her, and how through possession of the name she gained power over him and over all the other gods. In many other ways, too, Egyptian religious life in all its phases evinces over and over again this belief in the supremacy of the name and the magic power that dwells in it. The ceremonies attending the anointment of kings are governed by minute prescriptions for the transference of the god's several names to the Pharaoh; each name conveys a special attribute, a new divine power.

6. Moreover, this motive plays a decisive role in the Egyptian doctrines of the soul and its immortality. The souls of the departed, starting on their journey to the land of the dead, must be given not only their physical possessions, such as food and clothing, but also a certain outfit of a magical nature: this consists chiefly of the names of the gatekeepers in the nether world, for only the knowledge of these names can unlock the doors of Death's kingdom. Even the boat in which the dead man is conveyed, and its several parts, the rudder, the mast, etc., demand that he call them by their right names; only by virtue of this appellation can he render them willing and subservient and cause them to take him to his destination.

7. The essential identity between the word and what it denotes becomes even more patently evident if we look at it not from the objective standpoint, but from a subjective angle. For even a person's ego, his very self and personality, is indissolubly linked, in mythic thinking, with his name. Here the name is never a mere symbol, but is part of the personal property of its bearer; property which must be carefully protected, and the use of which is exclusively and jealously reserved to him. Sometimes it is not only his name, but also some other verbal denotation, that is thus treated as a physical possession, and as such may be acquired and usurped by someone else. Georg von der Gabelentz, in his book on the science of language, mentions the edict of a Chinese emperor of the third century B.C., whereby a pronoun in the first person, that had been legitimately in popular use, was henceforth reserved to him alone. And the name may even acquire a status above the more or less accessory one of a personal possession, when it is taken as a truly substantial Being, an integral *part* of its bearer. As such it is in the same category as his body or his soul. It is said of the Eskimos that for them man consists of three elements—body, soul, and name. And in Egypt, too, we find a similar conception, for there the physical body of man was thought to be accompanied, on the one hand, by his Ka, or double, and, on the other, by his name, as a sort of spiritual double. And of all these three elements it is just the last-mentioned which becomes more and more the expression of a man's "self," of his "personality." Even in far more advanced cultures this connection between name and personality continues to be felt. When, in Roman law, the concept of the "legal person" was formerly articulated, and this status was denied to certain physical subjects, those subjects were also denied official possession of a proper name. Under Roman law a slave had no legal name, because he could not function as a legal person.

8. In other ways, too, the unity and uniqueness of the name is not only a mark of the unity and uniqueness of the person, but actually constitutes it; the name is what first makes man an individual. Where this verbal distinctiveness is not found, there the outlines of his personality tend also to be effaced. Among the Algonquins, a man who bears the same name as some given person is regarded as the latter's other self, his alter ego. If, in accordance with a prevalent custom, a

child is given the name of his grandfather, this expresses the belief that the grandfather is resurrected, reincarnated in the boy. As soon as a child is born, the problem arises which one of his departed ancestors is reborn in him; only after this has been determined by the priest can the ceremony be performed whereby the infant receives that progenitor's name.

9. Furthermore, the mythic consciousness does not see human personality as something fixed and unchanging, but conceives every *phase* of a man's life as a new personality, a new self; and this metamorphosis is first of all made manifest in the changes which his name undergoes. At puberty a boy receives a new name, because, by virtue of the magical rites accompanying his initiation, he has ceased to exist as a boy, and has been reborn as a man, the reincarnation of one of his ancestors. In other cases the change of name sometimes serves to protect a man against impending danger; he escapes by taking on a different self, whose form makes him unrecognizable. Among the Evé it is customary to give children, and especially those whose elder brothers or sisters have died young, a name that has a frightful connotation, or attributes some non-human nature to them; the idea is that Death may be either frightened away, or deceived, and will pass them by as though they were not human at all. Similarly, the name of a man laboring under disease or bloodguilt is sometimes changed, on the same principle, that Death may not find him. Even in Greek culture this custom of altering names, with its mythic motivation, still maintained itself. Quite generally, in fact, the being and life of a person is so intimately connected with his name that, as long as the name is preserved and spoken, its bearer is still felt to be present and directly active. The dead may, at any moment, be literally "invoked," the moment those who survive him speak his name. As everyone knows, the fear of such visitation has led many savages to avoid not only every mention of the departed, whose name is tabooed, but even the enunciation of all assonances to his name. Often, for instance, an animal species whose name a defunct person had borne has to be given a different appellation, lest the dead man be inadvertently called upon by speaking of the beast. In many cases procedures of this sort, entirely mythic in their motivation, have had a radical influence on language, and modified vocabularies considerably. And the further a Being's power extends, the more mythic potency and "significance" he embodies, the greater is the sphere of influence of his name. The rule of secrecy, therefore, applies first and foremost to the Holy Name; for the mention of it would immediately release all the powers inherent in the god himself.

10. But here let us stop; for it is not our intention to collect theological or ethnological material, but to clarify and define the problem presented by such material. Such interweaving and interlocking as we have found between the elements of language, and the various forms of religious and mythical conception cannot be due to mere chance; it must be rooted in a common characteristic of language and myth as such. Some scholars have sought to base this intimate connection on the suggestive power of words, and especially of a spoken command, to which primitive man is supposed to be particularly subject; the magical and daemonic power which all verbal utterance has for the mythic state of consciousness seems to them to be nothing more than an objectification of that experience. But such a narrow empirical and pragmatic foundation, such a detail of personal or social experience, cannot support the prime and fundamental facts of linguistic and mythic conception. More and more clearly we see ourselves faced with the question whether the close relationship of contents which certainly obtains between language and myth may not be most readily explained by the common form of their evolution, by the conditions which govern both verbal expression and mythic imagination from their earliest, unconscious beginnings.

11. Preuss reports that, according to the Cora Indians and the Uitoto, the "Patriarch" created men and nature, but that since this creation he no longer interferes directly with the course of events. In lieu of such personal intervention, he gave to men his "Words," i.e., his cult and the religious ceremonies by means of which they now control nature and attain whatever is necessary for the welfare and perpetuation of the race. Without these holy spells which were originally given into their keeping, men would be entirely helpless, for nature yields nothing merely in return for human labor. Among the Cherokees, too, it is an accepted belief that success in hunting or fishing is due chiefly to the use of certain words, of the proper magic formulas.

12. Whatever has been fixed by a name, henceforth is not only real, but is Reality. The potential between "symbol" and "meaning" is resolved; in place of a more or less adequate "expression," we find a relation of identity, of complete congruence between "image" and "object," between the name and the thing.

5 of Worst Hurricanes 'Retired'

WASHINGTON—(UPI)— The Weather Bureau has retired for the next 10 years the names of five unusually destructive hurricanes that struck the United States in recent years.

In announcing names for storms in the 1967 season opening June 1, it has retired the names of Betsy, Connie, Diane, Hazel and Donna.

At the end of 10 years, the names will be returned to four alphabetical lists that are rotated each year.

This year's names are Arlene, Beulah, Chloe, Doria, Edith, Fern, Ginger, Heidi, Irene, Janice, Kristy, Laura, Margo, Nona, Orchid, Portia, Rachel, Sandra, Terese, Verna and Wallis.

UPI Dispatch, *San Francisco Chronicle,* Wednesday, May 31, 1967

There is no question in my mind why Parnelli Jones missed winning the Indianapolis Day-After-Memorial-Day 500 mile auto race.

Sure, I know the announced reason was that he had gear-box trouble in his four-wheel drive, turbine-powered whatchamacallit. But hell, who doesn't have gear-box trouble. Why, I once owned an MG sedan that . . . But why go into that?

Anyway, the real trouble, Parnelli, was not in the box but in the booth—the broadcasters' booth. Some lout up there lacking the remotest knowledge of the occult had the temerity to suggest that all Jones and his earthbound aircraft had to do was "roll in" to victory and $171,227. Furthermore, I understand, another blasphemous pronouncer suggested that with only a few laps to go the odds must be something like a million-to-one against a Jones loss.

Well, as everyone from H. P. Lovecraft to Anton LaVey will attest, that's just asking for it.

There isn't an engine manufactured—turbine or what-have-you—that can buck a jinx like that. Even those of us who don't dash about waving dirty sox stuffed with chicken livers at the moon know the fates should never be tempted. For if there is anyone they enjoy demolishing it's a smart-asinine blowhard.

I ask you, how many times has victory seemed within your clutches on the golf course, the paddle ball court or the marketplace, for that matter, when something mysterious snatches it away?

The magic words, of course, are, "I've got it made."

Heaven—or hell—knows what Jones might have been thinking as he purred home to a certain victory in that thing of his, but whatever it was, somebody up—or down—there heard him. And his doom was further sealed by the nationwide announcement that he was home free.

The fateful words were swallowed seconds after they escaped. "Hold on there, something's wrong, Jones is headed for the pits. . . ."

Sputter, sputter. . . . "Woo-ha-ha, the Shadow knows . . ."

Compare the Jones curse with A. J. Foyt's triumph. Foyt, who had twice won the Indianapolis race, understands life's little cruelties.

When the scent of victory first reached him, he promptly looked for trouble instead of the checkered flag. It was a devilishly wise thing to do, for just as he suspected, cars began to skid and crash in front of him like so many commuters on the Nimitz freeway.

"I figured, 'there it goes,' " he was quoted as saying after the great race. The "there" naturally being the $171,227 winner's purse.

It was the right thing to say, so he somehow weaved his way through the flying metal to the finish line.

I don't want anyone to misread this document as a treatise against self-confidence—only against over-confidence.

It's comforting to be sure of oneself, I am told by those lunatics who are. But even they recognize the folly of being too sure in a world alive with demons and gnomes.

Ron Fimrite, "You Asked For It,"

San Francisco Chronicle, June 1, 1967

We commonly say we feel a certain way about something, but what we say is neither the thing observed nor our feeling about it. In the following essay Wendell Johnson suggests that by ignoring these distinctions we may deceive ourselves. What, for example, do we refer to when we cite a "fact"? Is it an immutable fact of nature, a momentary fact, or only a partial and subjective observation? If by "fact" we mean "opinion," why do we distinguish between the two? In which ways are "facts" useful? Recognition of the difficulties inherent in all communication, even of facts, Johnson concludes, is the first step toward a more humane understanding.

The World of Not-Words

Wendell Johnson

It has been said by many, and in various ways, that the problems of knowing and of understanding center around the relation of language to reality, of symbol to fact. These ink marks over which your eyes are racing, these ink marks that we agree to call words, and these words that we agree to accept as "legal tender" for the exchange of information, by what magic, or by what humdrum rules, do they serve their strange functions? If you stare at a word long enough, it does

From *People in Quandaries* by Wendell Johnson, pp. 91-109. Copyright 1946 by Harper & Brothers. Reprinted by Harper & Row, Publishers.

indeed become, for you, mere ink marks, a peculiar pattern of lines. At first it looks as though it were spelled correctly, then you cannot be sure, and finally you are overcome with the feeling that to consider its spelling at all is to enter into the most entangled mazes of humanity.

2. Of course if you stare at anything sufficiently long and thoughtfully, as a calf stares at a new gate, it tends to appear as last as though it were utterly unaccountable. A great philosopher once remarked that the strangest invention in all history was that peculiar covering for the human foot that we call a sock. He had been looking at one for several minutes. There are times when it seems impossible, however, that any other human invention could be more astonishing and strange than a word—the word *sock*, for example.

3. One may wonder how words came to exist in the first place, and how they "get" their "meaning." One may wonder, as C. K. Ogden and I. A. Richards wondered throughout a sizable book, about "the meaning of meaning." And we can be sure that at least one would discover sooner or later that a word "means" something more than other words. People who are accustomed, for example, to look in a dictionary for the meanings of words proceed under a great delusion if they suppose that what they find in a dictionary is a word's full meaning. What they find is that the dictionary definition of a word consists of other words. Moreover, a dictionary is a closed system. In it, not only is a word defined in other words, but these, in their turn, are also defined in other words—and if you follow far enough this trail of definitions of words, you find that it is a trail that goes in a great circle, so that finally you make the enlightening discovery that the words are defined by each other. *Space* is defined in terms of *length* and *length* is defined in terms of *space*, *beauty* is defined in terms of *good* and *good* in terms of *beauty*, etc. When you have energetically explored a dictionary, what you know are words, and what you know about them are words, too. And if all you know are words, you are left with the question with which you started, the question of what words "mean"—besides other words.

4. The question is incredibly complex, and our stupidity has been expressed persistently in the unduly simple answers we have given to it. We can avoid a repetition of that stupidity, at least in part, by the easy means of announcing that we do not propose here to exhaust the subject. Our aims are modest. We are concerned chiefly with three

aspects of "meaning": with the non-verbal *facts* which words represent, with the *evaluations* which they express, and with the *effects* which they have on those who hear or read them, including their effects on the persons who speak or write them. The word *blonde*, for example, may refer to a particular person, or it may be spoken in such a way as to express evaluations ranging all the way from love to disgust, or its utterance may lead to any reaction from cheery smiles to homicide. What *blonde* "means" according to the dictionary is something else again, and it is not our primary concern. It is the primary concern of certain other students of language, and the work they do is important. Moreover, there are many other ways of considering the "meaning" of a word. The problem is as profound and as intricate as the problem of humanity itself. Certainly we shall not attempt to exhaust it. Within the limits of our major interests, however, we shall deal with it in an orderly way.

What Is a Fact?

5. Let us begin by looking briefly at the main steps involved in the seemingly simple process of Mr. A speaking to Mr. B—the process of communication. First, there is a "fact," which is to say that something happens to stimulate Mr. A. He feels it and interprets it. He speaks, verbalizing his interpretation. In speaking, Mr. A produces sound waves which serve to vibrate certain membranes and fluids in Mr. B's ear. This sets up activity in Mr. B's auditory nerve, and so in his brain cortex, and then he interprets what goes on in his cortex. Finally he says something or does something—to which Mr. A in turn reacts, and then Mr. B reacts again to Mr. A, etc. This sort of thing has been going on among hundreds of millions of people for thousands of years, with the result that human society has been growing more and more complex. Mr. A talking to Mr. B is a very important matter. Around it center practically all our problems of human understanding and disagreement, of cooperation and conflict, of knowledge and stupidity, of peace and war.

6. Just what goes on when Mr. A speaks to Mr. B? We said that, to begin with, there is a fact. It is this part of the process that we shall consider in the present chapter. The basic question we have to examine is simply this: What is a fact? Propaganda experts, so-called, keep warning us about the dangers of what they call emotional appeals. They urge us to look at the facts, to insist on the facts, to keep our eyes on the facts. This advice is so disarmingly simple. It leaves so much to chance, takes so much for granted. Behind it lies the assumption that a fact is a fact, and that everyone knows, a fact when he sees one. In the meantime, there are some very elementary considerations to be taken into account. One is that knowing the facts is impossible if one means knowing *all* the facts about anything. Whenever anyone advises you not to act until you know the facts, he puts you under a spell of inaction forever unless he indicates which facts and how many of them you are to know, because you will never know them completely. Then, too, what we call facts have a way of changing, so that yesterday's statistics become today's fairy tales. Furthermore, a fact appears different depending on the point of view; your facts are not exactly like those of someone else. Actually, one man's fact is not infrequently another man's fiction. This means, finally, that facts are, in important measure, a matter of social agreement. Unless these elementary points are clearly recognized, telling people to stick to the facts is usually a sure-fire way of getting them embroiled in hopeless argument.

7. If you would recognize a fact when you see one and make the most of it, there are, then, four things about any fact that you must be clear about: It is necessarily incomplete, it changes, it is a personal affair, and its usefulness depends on the degree to which others agree with you concerning it.

A fact is necessarily incomplete. There are definite limitations to our ability to observe the world about us, to say nothing of our ability to observe ourselves. There are certain air waves that we do not register as sound. There are energy radiations that we do not see, or feel, or in any other way recognize. In order to see beyond certain limits of magnitude we must use microscopes, and even microscopes have their limitations. In other words, we get only as much of the facts as we can with the sensory organs—and the magnifying devices—we have to work with. Beyond the directly observable lies the microscopic world, and beyond even that the submicroscopic realm extends to limits, if there are limits, that we can imagine scarcely better than a blind child can imagine the appearance of trees in autumn.

8. What we observe as a fact is necessarily an abstract, an expurgated version, so to speak, of something concerning which we can only conjecture. "If he is ingenious he may form some picture of a mechanism

which could be responsible for all the things he observes. . . ." Thus, indeed, and inescapably, "in our endeavor to understand reality we are somewhat like a man trying to understand the mechanism of a closed watch" which he has no way of opening. So far we may go and no farther in our explorations of reality. Our "facts" are incomplete. The argument against intolerance and dogmatism is not, in the final analysis, a "moral" argument; it rests solidly upon the simple consideration that it is humanly impossible to know *all* the facts, or even all of any one fact. The carrier of dogma is deluded; he may or may not be "immoral."

9. We can know something, however. Facts change, and yet a semblance of yesterday remains in today's sounds and visions. Facts change, but sufficient unto the day are the facts thereof. Indeed change itself would appear to be the most important fact of all. Facts as we observe them are little more than quick glimpses of a ceaseless transformation—as if we viewed the separate frames of a moving picture without quite realizing that what we were viewing was, in fact, a *moving* picture. Looking closely at a motion-picture film we see that each successive frame is slightly different from the last. Just so, looking closely at a "fact" we see that it appears slightly—or markedly—different from time to time. The grasses grow, the fruit ripens, the boy becomes a man. A person, as we know him, is a kind of average, a fusion or blending, an abstract, of many different observations that we have made of him. Like the sting of a bee, each fact occurs but once. Because *facts* change, any one fact is unique. Actually, to say that facts change is to say simply that no two facts are completely alike. Generally speaking, however, all the facts within our range do not change so utterly or so suddenly as to leave us dumb with surprise. True, there are times when change takes us quite unawares; that is the basis of comedy—and of tragedy. But so long as we remain responsive to the fact of change itself, the ever-changing facts are not, as a rule, unnerving.

10. In a basic sense a fact is an observation. An observation is the act of an individual. So it is that a fact is a personal affair. After all, that is why a fact (considered as a personal observation) is necessarily incomplete: The individual who observes it is limited in observational capacity. And that, in part, is why a fact changes: The individual who observes it is himself changing continuously, and so he observes differently from time to time. To paraphrase Heraclitus, the same man cannot step in a river twice. Having learned this lesson for the first time, we bewail our disillusionment, and having learned it well, we treasure our foresight. We do not merely discover facts; in some degree we fashion them. "The world as known to us is a joint product of the observer and the observed." The basic importance of the personal equation in what we call facts is illustrated in homely and effective terms in the following passage from the introductory chapter in the fifth volume of *Colloid Chemistry,* edited by Jerome Alexander:

> Lest we be too confident of all our sensory knowledge, let it be recalled that Blakeslee and Fox demonstrated that the ability of persons to taste phenylthiocarbamid is heritable as a Mendelian recessive, and that even those who get any taste at all from it (about 70 per cent) describe it variously as bitter, sweet, salty, or sour. This indicates that there is a relativity of sense impressions. H. C. Moir tested sixty persons as to their ability to recognize by taste four simple flavors—orange, lemon, lime, and vanilla. Only one person had a perfect score. Five had records of over 75 per cent, but forty-eight failed to reach 50 per cent. Vanilla was variously identified as black currant, lime, apricot, greengage, damson, lemon, pineapple, orange, tangerine, almond, red currant, strawberry. Only a limited number of persons can taste sodium benzoate, and wide differences exist in the ability to detect and recognize such odors as verbena and to distinguish between wines. R. J. Williams reports (*Science,* Dec. 11th, 1931) that a man whose sense of smell appeared otherwise normal could not detect the odor of a skunk, while n-butyl mercaptan, the "perfume" carried by skunks, had no unpleasant odor for him. Laselle and Williams in attempting to identify a substance as creatinine, found it tasteless, though the literature states that creatinine is bitter. It was not until they had tried the sample on several others that they located someone who found it bitter. Since lean meat contains much creatinine (about 2 grams per pound), and soups made from lean meat contain extracted creatinine, we have another possible basis of differences in taste. Williams believes that the problem is associated with the more general one of individual metabolic idiosyncrasies, which crop up at times in medicine (*e.g.,* reactions to morphine, novocaine, iodoform) or in industry (reactions to cosmetics, "chemicals," etc.).

11. There is, indeed, no accounting for taste, unless we recognize the fact that it is an individual matter in a fundamental physiological sense. And the individual differences, great as they are to begin with, become tremendously confounded when the factors of training, or so-called psychological conditioning, are brought into play. What is true in this respect of the sense of taste is likewise true in varying degrees of all the other sense modes. Individual differences in sensory capacity in its various aspects have been heavily documented by scientific investigators in many laboratories. This is to say that a fact, as an observation, is a personal affair, to be trusted as such and not as a universal truth.

12. What this means, in practical terms, is that a fact is useful, or dependable, to the degree that other persons agree with you concerning it. (We are referring here, of course, to first-order facts, not to conclusions that might be drawn from them. One man's conclusions can be better than those of the people who disagree with him.) If the majority say something is green every time you say it is red, you had best take their word for it. If a doctor, two internes, and a nurse all agree that there are no grasshoppers on your suit jacket, you might as well quit trying to brush them off. Generally speaking, the larger the number of people who agree as to a fact, the more dependable the fact is.

13. This is to be said, however, with two qualifications. The first is that some observers are more reliable than others. If you were a factory personnel manager hiring inspectors whose job was to detect flaws in metal plates, you would not employ applicants indiscriminately. In a sample pile of 100 metal plates there might be 27, for example, that were defective as determined by ten experienced inspectors. An applicant who would find only 17 or as many as 36 defective plates in the pile would not be as reliable an observer as one who would find 27. Modernized factories use various kinds of so-called aptitude tests in determining the reliability of applicants for work requiring observational ability. The general principle underlying such tests is that the reliability of an observer is to be measured in terms of his agreement with other observers. Fundamentally, what we mean by a good observer is one with whom other observers of experience and established competence tend to agree. It is not necessarily true that one man's report of a fact is as good as another's.

14. Another aspect of this general point is that agreement in making observations depends in part on similarity in the conditions under which they are made. If you have a microscope and I have none, you may disregard my disagreements with you. But if I use the same microscope as you, our disagreements become important. Every newly discovered microbe, every new synthetic substance, every newly dis-

covered fact of any sort is for a time known to only one person. No
one else may dispute it simply because others have not observed it, so
long as these others have not used the proper method for observing it.
Its dependability as a fact increases, however, as more and more other
persons do observe it. In fact, until it is observed by at least two individuals, it remains unsubstantiated. What all this amounts to is that
some observers are more reliable than others, not only because of differences in ability to use the same equipment and techniques, but also
because of differences in available equipment and technique.

15. The other qualification is that some observations simply cannot
be verified *directly* by a second party. If I tell you that I have a toothache, you have to take my word for it so far as any direct confirmation
by you is concerned. You cannot feel my toothache. Nor can I tell you
the toothache; I can only tell you about it. How, then, is a fact of this
sort to be verified? Indirectly. We commonly say, "He says he has a
toothache, but he doesn't act like it." Or "He says he has a headache,
but there certainly doesn't seem to be any reason for it." Physicians
distinguish two major types of condition of this kind: malingering and
hysteria. When a person says that he is unable to hear, he may be deaf
in the ordinary sense, but also he may be pretending (malingering), or
he may be suffering from hysterical deafness. The proper examination
methods give strong indirect evidence as to whether the condition is
one or the other of these types. Essentially, if it can be shown that the
accepted physical causes of deafness are absent and, further, that the
person can hear, we say he is malingering—not only is he giving a
false report, but he knows he is. If, however, the accepted physical
causes are absent and the person cannot hear, at least not under conditions sufficient to demonstrate hearing in a malingerer, we say he is
either genuinely deaf, or else hysterically deaf. Absence of the accepted or known physical causes of deafness is strong evidence that
he is not genuinely deaf, of course, but there remains in such a case
the possibility that medical history is on the verge of being made by
the discovery of some physical cause of deafness not previously recognized. Generally speaking, hysterical deafness is the diagnosis made
when, so far as can be determined, physical causes are absent and the
person is honest in reporting that he cannot hear. What we mean essentially by saying that a person is hysterically deaf is that, although
he has the physical equipment for hearing, he does not hear because of
emotional conflicts which make hearing intolerable for him. The fact

that, when the emotional conflicts are cleared, the person hears and freely admits it is taken as good evidence that he is not, or was not, malingering.

16. The report of any so-called inner experience—as of an ache, pain, itch, etc., that cannot be observed directly by a second party—may, then, be (a) reliable, (b) deliberately false, or (c) hysterical. Whether it is the one or the other has to be determined by indirect evidence. We accept it as reliable when it is consistent with the conditions and the behavior associated with it. Whether or to what degree it is consistent, and so reliable, depends, even in this case, on agreement among the persons who are in a position to observe its consistency.

With these qualifications granted, therefore, we may say that a fact is an observation agreed upon by two or more persons situated, qualified, and equipped to make it—and the more persons agreeing, the better.

The Process of Abstracting: Non-Verbal Levels

17. We have said, then, that a first-order fact, as an observation, is incomplete, an abstract of a fuller, more detailed reality which we can only partially observe directly. We have also said that observations made with the naked eye, as it were, can be extended by means of magnifying devices, such as microscopes, telescopes, high-speed cameras, etc. (We call these extra-neural means of observing, because they provide the nervous system with extra stimulation beyond that afforded by the unaided sense organs.)

18. A simple diagram will serve to summarize these statements. We shall begin by presenting only part of the diagram (Fig. 1), expanding it later and explaining it as we go along.

19. Figure 1 represents what we call facts in our common everyday speech. Facts, in this sense, are anything that we observe, anything that we see, hear, smell, taste, touch or feel kinaesthetically, internally. Thus, anything from a hippopotamus to a microbe, anything from a fever to an itch, is a fact, as here diagrammed, so long as it is directly experienced. The diagram represents two levels of facts: the macroscopic, or level of direct neural observation, and the microscopic, or level of extra-neural observation. We refer to these as levels of *abstraction,* because, as we have said, observations are necessarily

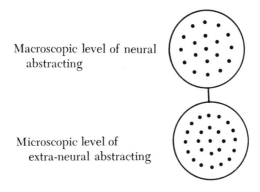

Macroscopic level of neural
abstracting

Microscopic level of
extra-neural abstracting

Figure 1. *Schematic diagram of macroscopic and microscopic levels
of abstraction.*

incomplete. They are abstracts, and observation is a process of abstracting.

20. We can make this more clear by adding a third level to our diagram (Fig. 2). The third, or lowest, level represents, in terms of Einstein and Infeld's analogy, "the mechanism inside the watch." It represents the reality that lies beyond the reaches of our observation, the submicroscopic realm, which we know only by inference. That is why we refer to it as the level of *inferential* data. The word *data* is important. It says that this submicroscopic realm is to be regarded as factual. From a scientific point of view, we talk about it in terms of atoms, electrons, etc., and our talk does not express mere fantasy. With it we make the best sense we can.

21. Suppose, for example, that you fill a glass with water and leave it on your desk. Now, you can observe the water in the glass just as it stands there, or you can place a droplet of it on a glass slide and view it under a microscope. On the basis of such observations you can say certain things about the water, and you will be "talking facts." One of the observations you will make, however, if you leave the water on your desk for a few days, is that the amount of it decreases. The glass does not leak, nobody drinks from the glass, you do not see the water leave. Yet it gradually disappears. You say this is a fact. You call it evaporation. If you are ingenious you may form some picture of a mechanism which could be responsible for evaporation. Scientists

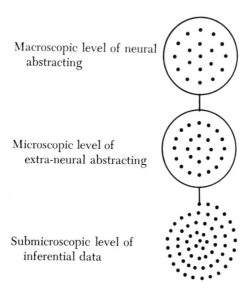

Macroscopic level of neural
abstracting

Microscopic level of
extra-neural abstracting

Submicroscopic level of
inferential data

Figure 2. Schematic diagram of non-verbal levels of abstraction.

have done so—in submicroscopic terms. Of course, you might "explain" evaporation in terms of unpredictable plogglies. Scientists explain it in terms of a molecular theory of matter. They *infer* that what we call water is made up of tiny particles in constant motion at high velocities. The particles, which they call molecules, are electrically charged so that they attract each other more or less, and partly for this reason most of them stay in the glass for several hours. A certain proportion of them, however, approach the surface of the water while moving at terrific speed and fly right out of the glass into the air. You don't see them go. They are too tiny to be seen. If the room is hot, the molecules in the glass move faster and so more of them fly out of the glass; and if the room becomes cold and the water freezes, this means that the molecules have slowed down a great deal and very few of them escape into the air. In other words, scientists do not merely say that there are molecules; they describe them—on the basis of inference, of course—in such a way as best to account for what they actually observe. By making their inferences this way, they can make predictions that would otherwise be impossible. With mere plogglies such predictions could not be made. Thus, having inferred that molecules have the properties which will account for increased evaporation at high temperatures, scientists can predict rates of evaporation at lower temperatures, or under different atmospheric pressures, etc. So often have scientists been able to verify predictions made on the basis of such inferences that they have built up elaborate dependable theories about the submicroscopic world of inferential data.

22. The development of the scientific theories which describe this vast submicroscopic world of inferential data is like a fascinating detective story serial, in many ways the most engrossing in our literature. It is the story of the creative imagining, later confirmed in many instances by actual discovery, not only of electrons, molecules, and atoms, but also of hormones, vitamins, antitoxins, bacteria, allergies. In the field of psychology the story has been worked out in terms of so-called unconscious conflicts, drives, wishes, and other mechanisms supposedly underlying our behavior. It has been worked out, too, in terms of motives, habit strengths, inhibitory states, and other inferential conditioners of learning and forgetting. From another direction the sleuths of science have moved in to discover chromosomes and genes, and so to write, paragraph by paragraph, the strange story of heredity. Growth and senility, health and disease, contentment and misery, genius and stupidity are understood today, insofar as they are understood at all, in terms not of facts in the ordinary sense, but of facts of an inferential kind.

23. In the most general sense, the submicroscopic realm is to be described in the dynamic terms of process, radiations, vibrations, a whirling dance of unobservable particles and wave motions. It is from this realm that we abstract the shadows and colors, the outlines and tangible facts that we know so incompletely, and sometimes misleadingly, through observation. And of these facts directly known to us, the most pervasive and the most dependable is the fact of change, seen as interminable array and never-ending series of differences, which we can know from experience and by which experience teaches us, if we permit it to teach us anything. By observing the differences and predicting the changes in the world about us and in ourselves, we learn, as well as we can, how to form a picture of a mechanism that will account for what we can observe. By forming such pictures and by revising them as our predictions prove false and our new observations disclose our old mistakes, we achieve increasingly an un-

derstanding of the facts with which we must daily contend. What this amounts to is that the significance of a fact lies chiefly in the theory by which we seek to explain it, for the theory by which we seek to explain it determines the use we will make of it.

24. There was a time, not so long ago, when even in the western world men assumed that insanity, for example, was to be accounted for on the basis of spirits and devils resident within the body of the afflicted individual. The observable facts of insane behavior were doubtless much the same then as now. What we do about those facts, however, is very considerably different today, and the reason for this is simply that today we no longer assume the presence of devils. The demonic plogglies have been replaced—not merely eliminated, but replaced—by other forms of inferential data, and correspondingly the older cruel methods of dealing with the insane have given way to more humane and more effective procedures. Even today psychiatrists differ in their methods of treating "mental" disease, because they differ in the assumptions which they employ in trying to account for it. Roughly, there are two major points of view. There are those, on the one hand, who lean toward the belief that insanity is hereditary, or that at least it is due primarily to so-called biological factors. On the other hand, there are those who favor the view that "mental" disease is primarily a product of training, or environmental factors. These two general types of theory, or inference, tend to result in different examination procedures, the making of different sets of observations, and different kinds of treatment. All of which is to emphasize that the significance of an observed fact lies mainly in the theory, the ultimate submicroscopic data, by which we seek to explain it.

25. For everyday practical purposes the most important consideration is simply this: the observations we make are incomplete. They are abstracted from something—from what we have represented in our diagram as the submicroscopic level of inferential data. We had best be aware, at least, of this general level of reality. We had best try, however crudely, to picture to ourselves what we assume it to be like. And if our picture does not serve to predict and account for the facts we do observe, we had best revise the picture. These are the minimum requirements for any person who would seek to behave scientifically, and to understand, even in an elementary fashion, the world about him and his own reactions to it.

26. It is to be noted that in our diagram we have placed a larger number of dots, representing details, in the microscopic circle than in the macroscopic circle. This is intended to indicate simply that with the unaided eye, or other sense organs, we cannot observe many aspects of an object or phenomenon which do become apparent to us when we employ extra-neural means or special techniques of observation. Water observed in the ordinary way may appear motionless and clear. A droplet of the "same" water viewed under a microscope would not appear so inert. We might see tiny forms of life darting about in it, for example. And if we were to place a pollen grain in the droplet we might observe the strange Brownian movement. . . .

27. The facts of human behavior, of anger, or weeping, or laughter, viewed without reference to the factors, the inferential factors, underlying them, can hardly be understood at all. On the basis of ordinary observation, such behavior can be described more or less, of course. The conditions under which it occurs can be described also, and a kind of explanation of our behavior can be made in terms of the conditions under which it occurs—of the stimuli to which we respond. Yet our observations of the behavior and of the stimulating conditions are so woefully incomplete that we can hardly achieve any significant understanding merely in terms of these observations, as such. As a matter of fact, whether or not we clearly realize it, we seldom state explanations of our actions simply by describing those actions or their environmental settings. We go beyond the obvious facts and attempt to account for our behavior in terms of "human nature," "heredity," "divine will," "instinct," "habit," etc.—or, in a more modern scientific way, we speak in more adequately defined terms of physiological, psychological and semantic factors, largely inferential. The consciousness of self, upon which personal adjustment ultimately depends, lies in a consciousness, a clear awareness, of the inferred factors, or assumptions, by which we try to understand ourselves. Unless we are clearly aware of these assumptions, we cannot be critical of them, we cannot test them and revise them so as to make them more useful in the prediction and control of our own behavior.

28. In order to test such an assumption, it is necessary to determine (a) how well it accounts for past behavior, (b) how well it enables you to predict future behavior, and (c) whether there are other factors or assumptions that make for better explanations and predictions. If, for example, you assume that your irritability in response to noise is hereditary, you will first of all recall as accurately as possible your past reactions to noise. Hereditary characteristics are by definition, relatively constant. The pattern of your fingerprints, the color of your eyes, the texture of your hair are presumably hereditary features, and they vary hardly at all from minute to minute or from year to year. If your reactions to noise vary considerably, you can hardly account for them, or predict them, in terms simply of heredity. Further study may indicate that your irritability is a learned reaction associated with only certain kinds of noise. Or perhaps you will discover that you are made irritable by noise only when you are hungry. A medical examination may reveal that you have stomach ulcers. If so, the physician will probably prescribe some form of treatment. If the treatment works, any understanding of why it works will depend upon the assumption of some kind of physico-chemical processes, for a full account cannot possibly be given in terms of what can actually be observed.

29. Thus, an object, or event, or human reaction, as observed directly on the macroscopic level, may be regarded as an abstract of what might be observed on the microscopic level. This is to say that our eyes do not give us a complete picture of an apple or a pencil, or a fit of anger, for example. And, as we have considered, the picture we get even on the microscopic level is likewise incomplete. It is an abstract of whatever there may be on the submicroscopic level. In our diagram we represent the submicroscopic level with a broken-line spiral in order to differentiate it sharply from the other two levels. The broken-line spiral is also intended to indicate the relatively more dynamic character of the inferred processes as compared with the facts which we abstract from them by observation. Moreover, our notions concerning the inferential data are not fixed with finality but are constantly held subject to revision; and we assume that the submicroscopic events serve to generate the differences and changes in reality as we observe it. All this we represent by the open end of the spiral and by drawing it with a broken instead of a solid line. It is to be noticed, too, that there are more "dots" in the spiral than in the circle above it. This is meant to indicate that even on the microscopic level we do not observe, or abstract, everything. Certain details are necessarily left out.

First-Order Facts

30. What we have represented on the macroscopic and microscopic levels may be regarded as first-order facts. What we mean by a first-order fact is simply a reliably observed fact. Objects fall, trees have bark, paper burns: these are first-order facts. There is a delightful little story for children in which this line recurs many times: "That is the way ducks do." The main character is a little yellow duck that swims, sticks its head under the water with its feet in the air, and in general carries on "the way ducks do." To the question, "Why do they?" a rather sensible answer, on the level of observable facts, is, "That is the way ducks do." It is a first-order fact about ducks. It states a norm. Why do we breathe, and why do our hearts beat? In a practical sense—that is to say, on the macroscopic and microscopic levels—there is no *why* about such things: they are simply first-order facts. Life and reality, as we experience them directly, are matters of first-order fact. Our ultimate understanding of life and reality, however, is basically in terms of the inferential processes by which we strive to account for first-order facts. It is extremely important, therefore, that we do not confuse our factual data with our inferential data.

31. We began our discussion by referring to the process of Mr. A speaking to Mr. B. This common and frequently momentous process begins properly with a fact. This is a way of saying that the study of language begins properly with a study of what language is about. The understanding of any symbol depends in large part upon a knowledge of what it symbolizes. In order to understand language it is necessary to know, at least in general terms, what it may be used to represent. That, essentially, is what we have been considering in terms of the macroscopic, microscopic, and submicroscopic levels—the non-verbal levels of abstracting.

How the Levels Differ

32. . . . Up to this point we have diagrammed what we might call the world of not-words. We have sketched a schematic representation of "reality," of the "physical world," of observable sense data, and of unobservable inferential data in terms of which we may know about the world in which we live and also about the life processes going on within ourselves. This world of not-words may be observed, or known, or abstracted, on different levels, of which we have recognized three for the purposes of our diagram.

33. There are certain summary statements to be made about these *levels of abstraction:*

34. One level is not the same as any other level. As we built up the diagram, we considered briefly how the levels differ, one from another, and these differences, as stated, seem quite obvious, no doubt. It is very important, however, that in regarding them as obvious we do not also regard them as of no particular significance. Our disposition to take such things for granted, without considering their consequences and implications, constitutes an important aspect of the semantic disorders which we shall take up in later chapters.

35. Some of the clear implications of the fact that one level of abstraction is not the same as any other level are to be seen in an investigation of what occurs when this fact is disregarded. And it is disregarded not only by the primitive who reacts to the inferential ghosts of his ancestors as though they were objective, live, present creatures, but also by the so-called "modern" individual who refuses to eat eggs, for example, because he evaluates the submicroscopic *process* egg as if it were the same as the macroscopic egg which he sees, smells, and tastes rarely if at all. Some persons should not eat certain foods because they are allergic to them, but ordinary food dislikes are as good an illustration as one could want of the confusion of one level of abstraction with another—of the failure, that is, to differentiate the levels, and to *act* as if one knew that the sense-data levels were different from the inferential-data level. We shall return to this point later. It is sufficient for the present to say only enough to give some significance to the basic statement that one level of abstraction is not the same as any other level.

36. The lower the level of abstraction, the more detailed and dynamic, the more process-like does reality appear to be. Thus, as we go to lower levels we gain a more nearly complete picture; we approach what Einstein and Infeld mean by the "ideal limit of knowledge"—we approach it but never reach it. We never reach it simply because we are physically limited, and also because we are investigating a process when we investigate reality or any phase of reality;

and before we could achieve *complete* knowledge of a process it would at least be necessary for the process to stop. But if we cannot achieve complete and final knowledge of the process which we call reality, at least the knowledge we can obtain can be kept relatively *up to date*. Moreover, an awareness, even a rough awareness, of the submicroscopic level of abstraction, as inferred by modern scientists, renders one less susceptible than one would otherwise be to believing all and only what one sees. To believe all one sees and that one sees all is to entertain sheer delusions. That such delusions may often be apparently harmless should not be permitted to obscure the plain fact that they are always potentially harmful and even disastrous. In certain "mental" diseases their effects are dramatically apparent.

37. *Abstractions on all these levels are unspeakable.* We can speak about them, but we can never transform them completely into words. A statement about direct experience can never be a duplicate of, or a full substitute for, the experience. Bite your tongue—not too hard. Now, try to *say* the feeling! Whatever you may say, the words you speak are not the feeling you speak about. The feeling, as such, is clearly *unspeakable*. This means, for example, that another person can never convey to us *all* that he feels, *all* that is occurring within him. He can only convey as much as words or other symbols will "carry." Therefore we can never be sure that we "know" how he feels. Recognition of this fact constitutes the very germ of anything we might call tolerance or humane understanding. Indeed, a consciousness of abstracting, as we shall see, gives a basis for a science of values, for adequate evaluation in social and personal affairs as well as in the physical sciences.

Although I believe that the table is 'really' of the same colour all over, the parts that reflect the light look much brighter than the other parts, and some parts look white because of reflected light. . . . if I move, the parts that reflect the light will be different, so that the apparent distribution of colours on the table will change. It follows that if several people are looking at the table at the same moment, no two of them will see exactly the same distribution of colours, because no two can see it from exactly the same point of view. . . . The same thing applies to the texture. With the naked eye one can see the grain, but otherwise the table looks smooth and even. If we looked at it through a microscope, we should see roughnesses and hills and valleys, and all sorts of differences that are imperceptible to the naked eye. Which of these is the 'real' table? We are naturally tempted to say that what we see through the microscope is more real, but that in turn would be changed by a still more powerful microscope. If . . . we cannot trust what we see with the naked eye, why should we trust what we see through a microscope?

Bertrand Russell,

*The Problems of Philosophy**

*Reprinted by permission of Oxford University Press.

In "Science and Linguistics" Benjamin Whorf suggests that the language of a culture shapes its attitudes and beliefs. In the following short essay John Lotz considers phenomena which might support Whorf's hypothesis. Stated targets for sports records (such as the four-minute mile) seem to depend much upon linguistic simplicity and a related simple conceptual organization. Why did the four-minute mile occupy public attention far more than, say, the three-minute fifty-eight second mile? Lotz concludes that the setting up of targets cannot be explained by non-linguistic references. Do you agree with his argument? If so, how much of your own life is similarly structured by your tendency to make linguistically simple and efficient formulations? While Lotz considers only one set of phenomena the implications are as broad as the title of his essay.

On Language and Culture

John Lotz

'Ideal targets' for records in sports provide a case-study in the currently fashionable discussion on the interrelation between language and culture. The difference between Anglo-Saxon countries and countries using the metric system may further elucidate the role of the linguistic factor.

2. In May 1954, when Bannister ran the 'dream mile' (one mile in less than 4 minutes), the newspapers listed a number of other ideal objec-

Reprinted from *International Journal of American Linguistics*, XXI, 1952, by permission of the publisher.

tives in sports: 9 seconds for the hundred-yard dash, 7 feet for the high-jump, 16 feet for the pole-vault, 60 feet for the shot-put (this one was achieved a few days later). These objectives were for male athletes; one can also add the 'dream mile' for women: one mile in less than 5 minutes (also reached in the same month).

3. All such 'ideals' aim at lowering the record time for running certain standard distances to a fixed number of seconds or minutes, or, in field events, at raising the length or height of the existing record to a fixed number of length units. The numbers involved are simple integers when the target number is low, and 'round figures' when the number is higher (4 minutes, 12 feet, 60 feet, but not 3¾ minutes for the mile or 61 feet for the shot-put). Such targets of course exist in other sports as well (e.g. in weight-lifting, or the 0.300 batting average in baseball).

4. That these targets depend on the use of language and not on other factors is demonstrated by the difference between the formulations of such targets in Anglo-Saxon countries and in countries using the metric system. The latter list as ideal targets: 10 seconds for 100 meters, 20 kilometers for the one-hour race, 80 meters for javelin-throwing, etc. Because of this dependence on language, such targets cannot be 'adequately' translated: to try to run 1603 meters in 4 minutes is not the same thing as shooting for the 4-minute mile.

5. These targets must be within reasonable reach, just above the present records, and therefore an ideal target can normally be formulated in only one measuring system; for instance in the high jump the target in Anglo-Saxon countries is 7 feet, half an inch above the present world record of 212 centimeters: 220, or even 225, is neither 'round' enough, nor realistic enough.

6. When such an ideal target is fashionable in the world of sports, as e.g., the 4-minute mile, the number of occasions on which that event is put on the program also increases (e.g., the one-mile race was often run in the 'metric' countries of Europe). When the ideal is achieved, that target gradually becomes obsolete; this has happened to the 30-minute 5 kilometers, and it will happen to the dream mile.

7. It seems clear that these ideal targets for sports records presuppose a general cultural setting of a non-verbal sort: appreciation of number and quantity, high valuation and meticulous recording of top physical performance, a realistic appraisal of man's physical abilities using the present top achievement as a reference point and extrapolating from there. But these targets must also be formulated verbally. The verbal

expression is an attribute phrase consisting of a number followed by measures of time, length, and weight. These expressions of the ideal targets readily lend themselves to analysis and interpretation by reason of their morphemic simplicity and semantic-conceptual transparency.

8. The second part of the verbal expression, the measure of time and length, is determined by tradition and convention. The foot-yard system, because of the larger number of basic units, allows a much greater variety of ideal targets than the metric system. The expressions for these measuring units are either single morphemes (second, minute, hour, inch, foot, year, mile, meter) or, in the metric system, consistently formed complex morphemes with a unifying stress pattern (centimeter, kilometer, etc.).

9. The number part of the phrase poses two linguistic problems with psychological and cultural implications: (a) the low, fundamental numbers, and (b) the round numbers.

10. The beginning of the integer series is said to be the cultural possession of all mankind, although in some cultures only the very first integers occur. They are single morphemes in English and in many languages. The round numbers, on the other hand, imply the selection of certain numbers, the base numbers, from the sequence of the integers (e.g., ten, a thousand, the '-illion' numbers, etc.), which make the manipulation of large numbers possible. The base numbers vary in different cultures (or they may be missing altogether); they may also vary within the same culture for different objects (e.g. in the Western culture twelve is used for eggs and paper; tjog *(twenty)* is used in Sweden for crayfish; the Akkadian 12 and 60 survive in time measures; in general use, the decimal system prevails in pure numbers, but not in measurements in Anglo-Saxon countries). Round numbers are either base numbers alone, or in simple combinations with the fundamental numbers. There are various degrees of 'roundness': any fundamental number in combination with any base number yields a round number (60,200,000, etc.); certain repetitive types, such as 110, 880, or the 666 of the Apocalyptic Beast, are also regarded as round, as are 5, 50, etc., and 25, 250, etc., in the decimal system. The feeling of what is round may vary in different countries, e.g. 16 is felt to be more round in Anglo-Saxon countries than in Continental Europe because it is a base in measurement—16 ounces to the pound. In all these numerical expressions the purely linguistic part is morphemically simple and the expression consists of a few differing morphemes: this is psychologically axiomatic; the reference, on the other hand, is determined by historical-cultural accident. The status of expression like quatre-vingt-dix *four score and ten,* and problems such as that of notation and its influence on the verbal expression are beyond the scope of these notes. (The counterpart of the round number is the simple fraction, especially binary divisions like half, quarter, etc., and in the decimal system the fractions ending in .5 or .25 etc., the decimal equivalents of successive halvings, which accounts for the feeling of roundness associated with 5, 25, etc. mentioned above).

11. The fundamental and the round numbers play a prominent part on the 'desiderative-imperative' aspects of our culture: in law, age limits, length of fish permitted to be caught, speed limits (with their implications for the problems of transportation); in sports: distances to be run specified in round numbers (the marathon distance, 26 miles, 385 yards, is a quasi-traditional distance introduced at the first Olympic Games); in social events: wedding anniversaries, college class reunions, bicentennials; in prices and salaries (the American $9.95 price tag is a deliberate avoidance of such numbers, aimed of course at having the customer psychologically class the article as within the range of the next lower 'round' price). In actual measurements, any degree of accuracy may be used that seems reasonable (running times are generally given in tenths of a second, distances in yards or fractions of miles; in the metric system, jumps and throws are measured only in whole centimeters), but even in actual reporting of numbers, rounding is common: on old tombstones ages are generally given in round tens, with fives next in frequency. Thus, it is the morphemic-conceptual simplicity and not the objective reference that is decisive.

12. The use of numbers in such targets determines cultural aims and behavior dependent on these. The simplicity of the linguistic expression and the correlated simple conceptual organization seem to account for the setting up of ideal aims and these cannot be explained by non-linguistic references, biological properties, or the like. The simplicity of the linguistic expression seems to be the organizing principle in other semantic fields also (such as colors, kinship, spatial organization, movements, etc.) in which simple morphemes or morpheme-combinations are set against expressions which might yield a more exact description and identification, but are linguistically complicated and cumbersome.

The runners matched each other stride for stride. At the last instant one dipped his head and snapped the tape. Both continued for 20 more yards, the anguish of the exertion etched on their faces.

Soon they sought each other, shook hands and slapped each other on the back. The 10th meeting between Northern California's best sprinters was over.

The race was won by Dave Masters, a curly, yellow-haired 17-year-old from El Cerrito High. His beaten foe was 18-year-old Mel Gray, a powerful youngster from Montgomery of Santa Rosa. Masters had just won his eighth race against Gray, but in this one both were timed the same, 9.5 seconds for the 100-yard dash.

Tim Gartner,

San Francisco Chronicle, May 25th, 1967

2

The Uses of Language

We incline to think of our Western view of time and space as somehow "objective." But is it in fact? To what extent do different languages determine different views of the world? If we spoke a different language, would we see the physical world differently?

In the present essay Whorf points out that in the language of the Hopi Indians there is no way of naming or making direct reference to "time," "past," "present," or "future." And yet the Hopi view of the universe may be no more or less objective than our own. Despite its mingling and apparently confusing concepts as basic to us as time and space, Hopi language serves Hopis as well as English serves us. In order that we may see this Whorf asks us to suspend for a short time our faith in the "objectivity" of our own world-view and to accept at least provisionally the adequacy of another, no matter how alien and strange it will at first seem.

An American Indian Model of the Universe

Benjamin Whorf

I find it gratuitous to assume that a Hopi who knows only the Hopi language and the cultural ideas of his own society has the same notions, often supposed to be intuitions, of time and space that we have,

Reprinted from *Language, Thought, and Reality* by Benjamin Lee Whorf by permission of The M.I.T. Press, Cambridge, Massachusetts. Copyright © 1956 by The Massachusetts Institute of Technology.

and that are generally assumed to be universal. In particular, he has no general notion or intuition of TIME as a smooth flowing continuum in which everything in the universe proceeds at an equal rate, out of a future, through a present, into a past; or, in which, to reverse the picture, the observer is being carried in the stream of duration continuously away from a past and into a future.

2. After long and careful study and analysis, the Hopi language is seen to contain no words, grammatical forms, constructions or expressions that refer directly to what we call "time," or to past, present, or future, or to enduring or lasting, or to motion as kinematic rather than dynamic (i.e. as a continuous translation in space and time rather than as an exhibition of dynamic effort in a certain process), or that even refer to space in such a way as to exclude that element of extension or existence that we call "time," and so by implication leave a residue that could be referred to as "time." Hence, the Hopi language contains no reference to "time," either explicit or implicit.

3. At the same time, the Hopi language is capable of accounting for and describing correctly, in a pragmatic or operational sense, all observable phenomena of the universe. Hence, I find it gratuitous to assume that Hopi thinking contains any such notion as the supposed intuitively felt flowing of "time," or that the intuition of a Hopi gives him this as one of its data. Just as it is possible to have any number of geometries other than the Euclidean which give an equally perfect account of space configurations, so it is possible to have descriptions of the universe, all equally valid, that do not contain our familiar contrasts of time and space. The relativity viewpoint of modern physics is one such view, conceived in mathematical terms, and the Hopi Weltanschauung is another and quite different one, nonmathematical and linguistic.

4. Thus, the Hopi language and culture conceal a METAPHYSICS, such as our so-called naïve view of space and time does, or as the relativity theory does; yet it is a different metaphysics from either. In order to describe the structure of the universe according to the Hopi, it is necessary to attempt—insofar as it is possible—to make explicit this metaphysics, properly describable only in the Hopi language, by means of an approximation expressed in our own language, somewhat inadequately it is true, yet by availing ourselves of such concepts as we have worked up into relative consonance with the system underlying the Hopi view of the universe.

5. In this Hopi view, time disappears and space is altered, so that it is no longer the homogeneous and instantaneous timeless space of our supposed intuition or of classical Newtonian mechanisms. At the same time, new concepts and abstractions flow into the picture, taking up the task of describing the universe without reference to such time or space—abstractions for which our language lacks adequate terms. These abstractions, by approximations of which we attempt to reconstruct for ourselves the metaphysics of the Hopi, will undoubtedly appear to us as psychological or even mystical in character. They are ideas which we are accustomed to consider as part and parcel either of so-called animistic or vitalistic beliefs, or of those transcendental unifications of experience and intuitions of things unseen that are felt by the consciousness of the mystic, or which are given out in mystical and (or) so-called occult systems of thought. These abstractions are definitely given either explicitly in words—psychological or metaphysical terms—in the Hopi language, or, even more, are implicit in the very structure and grammar of that language, as well as being observable in Hopi culture and behavior. They are not, so far as I can consciously avoid it, projections of other systems upon the Hopi language and culture made by me in my attempt at an objective analysis. Yet, if MYSTICAL be perchance a term of abuse in the eyes of a modern Western scientist, it must be emphasized that these underlying abstractions and postulates of the Hopian metaphysics are, from a detached viewpoint, equally (or to the Hopi, more) justified pragmatically and experientially, as compared to the flowing time and static space of our own metaphysics, which are *au fond* equally mystical. The Hopi postulates equally account for all phenomena and their interrelations, and lend themselves even better to the integration of Hopi culture in all its phases.

6. The metaphysics underlying our own language, thinking, and modern culture (I speak not of the recent and quite different relativity metaphysics of modern science) imposes upon the universe two grand COSMIC FORMS, space and time; static three-dimensional infinite space, and kinetic one-dimensional uniformity and perpetually flowing time —two utterly separate and unconnected aspects of reality (according to this familiar way of thinking). The flowing realm of time is, in turn, the subject of a threefold division: past, present, and future.

7. The Hopi metaphysics also has its cosmic forms comparable to these in scale and scope. What are they? It imposes upon the universe

two grand cosmic forms, which as a first approximation in terminology
we may call MANIFESTED and MANIFESTING (or, UNMANIFEST) or, again,
OBJECTIVE and SUBJECTIVE. The objective or manifested comprises all
that is or has been accessible to the senses, the historical physical universe, in fact, with no attempt to distinguish between present and
past, but excluding everything that we call future. The subjective or
manifesting comprises all that we call future, BUT NOT MERELY THIS;
it includes equally and indistinguishably all that we call mental—
everything that appears or exists in the mind, or, as the Hopi would
prefer to say, in the HEART, not only the heart of man, but the heart
of animals, plants, and things, and behind and within all the forms
and appearances of nature in the heart of nature, and by an implication and extension which has been felt by more than one anthropolo-
gist, yet would hardly ever be spoken of by a Hopi himself, so charged
is the idea with religious and magical awesomeness, in the very heart
of the Cosmos, itself.* The subjective realm (subjective from our
viewpoint, but intensely real and quivering with life, power, and
potency to the Hopi) embraces not only our FUTURE, much of which
the Hopi regards as more or less predestined in essence if not in exact
form, but also all mentality, intellection, and emotion, the essence
and typical form of which is the striving of purposeful desire, intelligent in character, toward manifestation—a manifestation which is
much resisted and delayed, but in some form or other is inevitable.
It is the realm of expectancy, of desire and purpose, of vitalizing life,
of efficient causes, of thought thinking itself out from an inner realm
(the Hopian HEART) into manifestation. It is in a dynamic state, yet
not a state of motion—it is not advancing toward us out of a future,
but ALREADY WITH US in vital and mental form, and its dynamism is
at work in the field of eventuating or manifesting, i.e., evolving without motion from the subjective by degrees to a result which is the
objective. In translating into English, the Hopi will say that these
entities in process of causation 'will come' or that they—the Hopi—
'will come to' them, but, in their own language, there are no verbs corresponding to our 'come' and 'go' that mean simple and abstract
motion, our purely kinematic concept. The words in this case trans-

---

*This idea is sometimes alluded to as the 'spirit of the Breath' (*hikwsu*) and as the
'Mighty Something' (*ʔaʔne himu*), although these terms may have lower and less
cosmic though always awesome connotations. [*Whorf's note*]

lated 'come' refer to the process of eventuating without calling it motion—they are 'eventuates to here' *(pew'i)* or 'eventuates from it' *(angqö)* or 'arrived' *(pitu,* pl. *öki)* which refers only to the terminal manifestation, the actual arrival at a given point, not to any motion preceding it.

8. This realm of the subjective or of the process of manifestation, as distinguished from the objective, the result of this universal process, includes also—on its border but still pertaining to its own realm—an aspect of existence that we include in our present time. It is that which is beginning to emerge into manifestation; that is, something which is beginning to be done, like going to sleep or starting to write, but is not yet in full operation. This can be and usually is referred to by the same verb form (the EXPECTIVE form in my terminology of Hopi grammar) that refers to our future, or to wishing, wanting, intending, etc. Thus, this nearer edge of the subjective cuts across and includes a part of our present time, viz. the moment of inception, but most of our present belongs in the Hopi scheme to the objective realm and so is indistinguishable from our past. There is also a verb form, the INCEPTIVE which refers to this EDGE of emergent manifestation in the reverse way—as belonging to the objective, as the edge at which objectivity is attained; this is used to indicate beginning or starting, and in most cases there is no difference apparent in the translation from the similar use of the expective. But, at certain crucial points, significant and fundamental differences appear. The inceptive, referring to the objective and result side, and not like the expective to the subjective and causal side, implies the ending of the work of causation in the same breath that it states the beginning of manifestation. If the verb has a suffix which answers somewhat to our passive, but really means that causation impinges upon a subject to effect a certain result —i.e., 'the food is being eaten,' then addition of the INCEPTIVE suffix in such a way as to refer to the basic action produces a meaning of causal cessation. The basic action is in the inceptive state; hence whatever causation is behind it is ceasing; the causation explicitly referred to by the causal suffix is hence such as WE would call past time, and the verb includes this and the incepting and the decausating of the final state (a state of partial or total eatenness) in one statement. The translation is 'it stops getting eaten.' Without knowing the underlying Hopian metaphysics, it would be impossible to understand how the same suffix may denote starting or stopping.

9. If we were to approximate our metaphysical terminology more closely to Hopian terms, we should probably speak of the subjective realm as the realm of HOPE or HOPING. Every language contains terms that have come to attain cosmic scope of reference, that crystallize in themselves the basic postulates of an unformulated philosophy, in which is couched the thought of a people, a culture, a civilization, even of an era. Such are our words 'reality, substance, matter, cause,' and as we have seen 'space, time, past, present, future.' Such a term in Hopi is the word most often translated 'hope'—*tunátya*—'it is in the action of hoping, it hopes, it is hoped for, it thinks or is thought of with hope,' etc. Most metaphysical words in Hopi are verbs, not nouns as in European languages. The verb *tunátya* contains in its idea of hope something of our words 'thought,' 'desire,' and 'cause,' which sometimes must be used to translate it. The word is really a term which crystallizes the Hopi philosophy of the universe in respect to its grand dualism of objective and subjective; it is the Hopi term for SUB-JECTIVE. It refers to the state of the subjective, unmanifest, vital and causal aspect of the Cosmos, and the fermenting activity toward frui-tion and manifestation with which it seethes—an action of HOPING; i.e. mental-causal activity, which is forever pressing upon and into the manifested realm. As anyone acquainted with Hopi society knows, the Hopi see this burgeoning activity in the growing of plants, the forming of clouds and their condensation in rain, the careful planning out of the communal activities of agriculture and architecture, and in all human hoping, wishing, striving, and taking thought; and as most especially concentrated in prayer, the constant hopeful praying of the Hopi community, assisted by their exoteric communal ceremonies and their secret, esoteric rituals in the underground kivas—prayer which conducts the pressure of the collective Hopi thought and will out of the subjective into the objective. The inceptive form of *tunátya*, which is *tunátyava*, does not mean 'begins to hope,' but rather 'comes true, being hoped for.' Why it must logically have this meaning will be clear from what has already been said. The inceptive denotes the first appearance of the objective, but the basic meaning of *tunátya* is sub-jective activity or force; the inceptive is then the terminus of such activity. It might then be said that *tunátya* 'coming true' is the Hopi term for objective, as contrasted with subjective, the two terms being simply two different inflectional nuances of the same verbal root, as the two cosmic forms are the two aspects of one reality.

10. As far as space is concerned, the subjective is a mental realm, a realm of no space in the objective sense, but it seems to be symbolically related to the vertical dimension and its poles the zenith and the underground, as well as to the 'heart' of things, which corresponds to our word 'inner' in the metaphorical sense. Corresponding to each point in the objective world is such a vertical and vitally INNER axis which is what we call the wellspring of the future. But to the Hopi there is no temporal future; there is nothing in the subjective state corresponding to the sequences and successions conjoined with distances and changing physical configurations that we find in the objective state. From each subjective axis, which may be thought of as more or less vertical and like the growth-axis of a plant, extends the objective realm in every physical direction, though these directions are typified more especially by the horizontal plane and its four cardinal points. The objective is the great cosmic form of extension; it takes in all the strictly extensional aspects of existence, and it includes all intervals and distances, all seriations and number. Its DISTANCE includes what we call time in the sense of the temporal relation between events which have already happened. The Hopi conceive time and motion in the objective realm in a purely operational sense—a matter of the complexity and magnitude of operations connecting events— so that the element of time is not separated from whatever element of space enters into the operations. Two events in the past occurred a long 'time' apart (the Hopi language has no word quite equivalent to our 'time') when many periodic physical motions have occurred between them in such a way as to traverse much distance or accumulate magnitude of physical display in other ways. The Hopi metaphysics does not raise the question whether the things in a distant village exist at the same present moment as those in one's own village, for it is frankly pragmatic on this score and says that any 'events' in the distant village can be compared to any events in one's own village only by an interval of magnitude that has both time and space forms in it. Events at a distance from the observer can only be known objectively when they are 'past' (i.e. posited in the objective) and the more distant, the more 'past' (the more worked upon from the subjective side). Hopi, with its preference for verbs, as contrasted to our own liking for nouns, perpetually turns our propositions about things into propositions about events. What happens at a distant village, if actual (objective) and not a conjecture (subjective) can be known 'here' only later. If it does not happen 'at this place,' it does not happen 'at this time'; it happens at 'that' place and at 'that' time. Both the 'here' happening and the 'there' happening are in the objective, corresponding in general to our past, but the 'there' happening is the more objectively distant, meaning, from our standpoint, that it is further away in the past just as it is further away from us in space than the 'here' happening.

11. As the objective realm displaying its characteristic attribute of extension stretches away from the observer toward that unfathomable remoteness which is both far away in space and long past in time, there comes a point where extension in detail ceases to be knowable and is lost in the vast distance, and where the subjective, creeping behind the scenes as it were, merges into the objective, so that at this inconceivable distance from the observer—from all observers—there is an all-encircling end and beginning of things where it might be said that existence, itself, swallows up the objective and the subjective. The borderland of this realm is as much subjective as objective. It is the abysm of antiquity, the time and place told about in the myths, which is known only subjectively or mentally—the Hopi realize and even express in their grammar that the things told in myths or stories do not have the same kind of reality or validity as things of the present day, the things of practical concern. As for the far distances of the sky and stars, what is known and said about them is supposititious, inferential—hence, in a way subjective—reached more through the inner vertical axis and the pole of the zenith than through the objective distances and the objective processes of vision and locomotion. So the dim past of myths is that corresponding distance on earth (rather than in the heavens) which is reached subjectively as myth through the vertical axis of reality via the pole of the nadir—hence it is placed BELOW the present surface of the earth, though this does not mean that the nadir-land of the origin myths is a hole or cavern as we should understand it. It is *Palátkwapi* 'At the Red Mountains,' a land like our present earth, but to which our earth bears the relation of a distant sky—and similarly the sky of our earth is penetrated by the heroes of tales, who find another earthlike realm above it.

12. It may now be seen how the Hopi do not need to use terms that refer to space or time as such. Such terms in our language are recast into expressions of extension, operation, and cyclic process provided they refer to the solid objective realm. They are recast into expressions of subjectivity if they refer to the subjective realm—the future, the psychic-mental, the mythical period, and the invisibly distant and conjectural generally. Thus, the Hopi language gets along perfectly without tenses for its verbs.

One widespread misconception is that certain languages are unaware of time, since they do not belong to the family of inflected languages and do not seem to have verbs. The underlying assumption here is that only verbs can express time. This argument contains a number of misconceptions which must be exposed. The verb-category can be recognized even in non-inflected languages, and time can be expressed in all types of linguistic structures. The paradigmatic organization particular to the tense-forms of certain languages, especially the Indo-European languages French, German, English, Spanish, etc. cannot claim, either in principle or in reality, the unique privilege of expressing time.

More general and more understandable is the misconception, nourished by man's propensity to regard language as the faithful mirror of reality, that the temporal system of a language reproduces the nature of "objective" time. What languages offer us in fact is only diverse constructions of reality, and it is perhaps precisely in elaborating a complex temporal system that languages diverge most radically from each other. We must ask ourselves at what level of linguistic expression we can reach the notion of time which necessarily imbues all languages and how this notion can be characterized.

Emile Benveniste,

"Language and Human Experience," *Diogenes* LI (Fall, 1965)

. . . But the outside world, i.e., the world of denotata can be approached not only through the categories of meaning but also direct. We not only acquire the knowledge that fire is hot through the words "warm," "hot," etc., in the mother tongue which accumulates the experience of many former generations, but also through the experience of burning our hand in childhood. Although the world of meanings is different and theoretically incomparable and incommensurable from one nation to another, the denotata amongst which people live are, in fact, the same for all humanity, or, at least, for a great number of people.

Laszlo Antal,

Questions of Meaning

One point is beyond doubt: the ready-made system of language determines our vision of the world in some way. If we do not have one term for snow, *we do not produce* the different kinds of snow in an arbitrary way. These exist in nature in an *objective* manner (though we might not have paid attention to them, when we concentrated on the properties common to all the kinds of snow, its color, temperature, etc.). It is not in the least a matter of convention that a given human community includes them in its vocabulary. Life itself required them. Distinguishing between various kinds of snow has been a matter of life and death for the members of that community. Practical activity contributed to the evolution of a given language; and the social experience fixed in language dominates the minds of the members of the given human community. The Eskimos *see* thirty kinds of snow, and not snow "in general," not because they want to do so, or because they have agreed to do so, but because they are unable to perceive reality in any other way.

Adam Schaff,

"Language and Reality," *Diogenes* LI (Fall, 1965)

We have to accept the fact that there are no such distinct meanings as "blue" and "green" in the Navaho language. But this does not mean that in the reality surrounding the Navahos there is no blue and green colour, or that from the standpoint of language green and blue could not be denotata. And, if, through the medium of their language, the Navajos cannot grasp the difference between green and blue, they can still see it with their eyes, that is, by their direct experience, just as we Europeans can divide into nuances that section of the spectrum which should be seen as uniformly black on the basis of the meanings of our respective languages.

Alternatively, let us examine the case of the tense system in the Hopi language. Although, in the Hopi language, at the meaning level, past, present and future are not distinguished, in reality the Hopi knows that something happened before or will happen afterwards.

Laszlo Antal,

Questions of Meaning

Naive realism, as distinguished from critical realism, asserts that things are as they seem to be, and that sensory qualities are inherent in the things themselves. We know that neither of these statements is tenable. Things *are not* as they seem to be. An analysis of common errors in perception reveals this fact. And science is constantly demonstrating the distance between our everyday image of the world, and the microscopic and macroscopic image provided by additional instruments. Sensory qualities *are not inherent* in things themselves. Perception depends on the perceiving apparatus.

Adam Schaff,

"Language and Reality," *Diogenes* LI (Fall, 1965)

As its title suggests, the following essay by Charles Hockett is an evaluation of Whorf's theses, set forth in "Science and Linguistics." Hockett's approach is simple and direct. Whorf has concluded that linguistic patterns, the form of language, structure semantic patterns, the form of thought. If he is right, Hockett reasons, then one expects to find that when a Chinese speaker says HWOCHE (from HWO 'fire' and CHE 'car' or 'cart') for "railroad train" (the dictionary translation of HWOCHE) he means something different from TRAIN—that the speaker of Chinese may imagine a cart spitting fire as it goes down the tracks. Without rejecting Whorf's hypotheses outright, Hockett disagrees. After considering a number of contrastive linguistic forms he concludes that the real case may be more complex. Perhaps there is more than one kind of difference between one language and another. Are some easier to isolate than others? Do all language-forms determine what CAN be said, or do they rather determine what is easy to say and what is difficult? To what extent must the student of language take into account the kinds of activity which language refers to?

Chinese Versus English: An Exploration of the Whorfian Theses (II)

Charles F. Hockett

Here we shall examine a number of points of difference between Chinese and English—with no effort to avoid the trivial—to see whether that particular pair of languages, contrastively examined, can shed any light on Whorf's theses. We are concerned largely with

Reprinted from *Language in Culture*, edited by Harry Hoijer, by permission of University of Chicago Press.

colloquial forms of the two languages, on the assumption that "thinking in words" is more apt to be colloquial than literary. Chinese is represented by the variety of northern Mandarin spoken by educated people in Peiping; citation is in Yale Romanization. For consistency and clarity, cited Chinese forms are italicized, while both English glosses and cited English forms are placed between quotation marks.

2. TRAINS. *Hwǒchē* '(railroad) train'; *hwǒ* 'fire'; *chē* 'car, cart, wheeled vehicle'. The tendency, in talking in English about the Chinese words just listed, is to say something like "Chinese *hwǒchē*, the word for 'train', means literally 'fire-cart' ". Now we can be sure of two things:

(1) When steam rail transportation was introduced into China, the term *hwǒchē* came into use because of the fire-spitting locomotive;

(2) The formal structure of *hwǒchē* is still validly to be described as a compound of *hwǒ* and *chē*, as listed and glossed above.

3. However, the remark given in double quotes above is misleading. Currently, *hwǒchē* means almost exactly what 'train' means—there is no necessary image of a fire-spitting locomotive inside the speaker's head when he uses or hears the word. Evidence for this is that 'electric train' (as on an electrified railroad) is *dyànlì-hwǒchē*, where *dyànlì* means 'electric power'; such a train does not have a fire-spitting locomotive.

4. This first example is given to illustrate the danger inherent in a study of this kind when the non-active language is not thoroughly controlled—a danger not altogether avoided in the present study, though all points made have been carefully checked with native speakers of Chinese whose control of English is considerably better than the writer's control of Chinese. What is apt to be called the "literal" meaning of a Chinese (or other) form in terms of English is very often the poorest possible basis for any judgment. No doubt the childish errors of nineteenth-century European students of comparative semantics stemmed from just such a basis: for example, the oft-repeated assertion that the Algonquians can say 'my father', 'thy father', or 'his father', but have no way of saying just 'a father', and hence "lack powers of abstraction."

5. CITIES AND WALLS. *Chyáng* 'wall (of a room, house, city)'; *chéng* 'city, city wall'; *chéngshr* 'city, municipality'; *chéngchyáng* 'city wall'; *dzài chéngli* 'be in the city'; *dzài chéngwài* 'be outside the city, be in the outskirts'; *cháng* 'long'; *wànli* 'ten thousand Chinese miles'; *chángchéng* or *wànli chángchéng* 'The Great Wall'. The form that is central

to our interest is *chéng*. The range of meaning of this element cannot be understood in terms of Western culture, but is immediately obvious when we recall that Chinese cities (except Shanghai) are universally enclosed in a square wall. With the exception of Shanghai, a clustering of dwellings and other structures which is not so enclosed is not a *chéng*, but a *tswēndz*, which we can gloss as 'village' if we are willing to redefine the English word for the purpose.

6. Here is a correlation between a particular segment of Chinese culture other than language and certain semantic features of the language. The correlation is different from that found in the English-speaking community. We fully expect that any two languages, chosen at random, will display a welter of such low-level differences; indeed, an exact match is a rarity worthy of notice.

7. AGE. In stating a person's age in English we use a cardinal number, followed, if necessary for clarity, by 'years old' or 'years of age'. In Chinese, one uses a cardinal number followed by the measure *swèi*. The possible matchings of English and Chinese expressions under various conditions can be shown as follows—where in English we assume that age is given to nearest birthday:

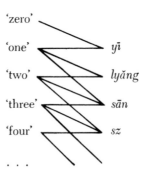

The absence of exact matching can be accounted for in terms of the meaning of the measure *swèi*. We can describe this as 'number of calendar years during all or part of which one has been alive'. In either language one can be far more precise in stating an age than these most customary expressions allow; in both languages the age of an infant is usually given in months, or months and days, rather than by any approximate formula. There are perhaps fewer occasions in Chinese culture in which such precision is called for than there are in English culture. To say 'so-many-years old' in Chinese, *swèi* in English, is possible but awkward. In ordinary usage one way of stating approximate age is as accurate, by and large, as the other.

8. Yet many Western scholars, approaching Chinese with too large a dose of glottocentrism, have passed snap judgment on the Chinese habit by saying something like, "In China [or: In Chinese] you are a year old when you are born."

9. FRUITS AND NUTS. If one has just eaten some strawberries, one can report the event in English by saying 'I just had some ——', filling the blank with 'strawberries', 'berries', 'fruit', or perhaps (this will not concern us) some even more generic term such as 'food'. A similar frame in Chinese, reporting the same event, could be filled with *yángméi* or *tsăuméi*, with *shwĕigwŏ*, or with *gwŏ*. In both languages the terms listed are idiomatic, not nonce-formations or especially coined descriptions. They line up as follows:

'strawberries'	*yángméi, tsăuméi*
'berries'	——
'fruit'	*shwĕigwŏ*
——	*gwŏ*

By this alignment we mean to indicate, for example, that 'berries' is a more inclusive term than *yángméi* or *tsăuméi*, but less inclusive than *shwĕigwŏ*.

10. Here there is close matching only at the most specific level. One can coin an expression in Chinese which will describe what 'berries' means in English; the expression is necessarily fairly long. Similarly, *gwŏ* can be paraphrased in English as 'fruits and/or nuts'. Neither the Chinese paraphrase for 'berries' nor the English paraphrase for *gwŏ* would ever naturally be used in the framework listed earlier. 'Strawberry' is a compound: it designates a kind of berry, and 'berry' is a single morpheme. *yángméi* and *tsăuméi* are both compounds, designating (the same kind of) *méi*, but *méi* does not mean 'berry'. This particular morpheme *méi*, in fact, does not occur as a whole word; there is a homophonous morpheme *méi* which does occur alone and which means something like 'plum'.

11. Where English has a single morpheme 'fruit', Chinese uses a compound *shwĕigwŏ* 'moist or watery *gwŏ*'. *Gwŏ* which is not *shwĕigwŏ* is *gāngwŏ* 'dry *gwŏ*', but this does not match the English 'nuts', since *gāngwŏ* includes both nuts and dried fruits. Finally, there is no close match in Chinese for English 'nuts'.

12. The hierarchy of terms for specific items and various more inclusive classes of items, illustrated here in the field of fruits and nuts, is in any given language the product of a vast number of historical accidents; identical coverage of generic terms in two unrelated languages would be a second-order accident. There is a special idiom within the general framework of most Western languages in which the effect of these accidents is removed and categorization is based on actual structural similarities. This is the idiom of science—for fruits and nuts, the terminology of botanical taxonomy. Botanically speaking, the class of items which in everyday parlance are called 'berries' does not constitute a meaningful category. The idiom of science constantly replaces haphazard classification by more objective ones. It is to be doubted whether any one language equips its speakers better than any other for the kind of semantic purification which the scientific approach necessitates. The Whorf approach suggests the value to an individual of learning a language of a type really alien to that of his own as a "second window" through which to view the universe. One may suspect that scientifically oriented study of the world about us is a more fruitful and enlightening experience of this sort than any study of a second language.

13. RANDOM HOLES IN PATTERNS. In any language we can expect to find points on which the grammatical pattern is such as to make speech awkward. In English it is difficult to ask an ordinary colloquial negative question with subject pronoun 'I' and verb 'be' in the present tense. In the past tense it is easy enough: 'Wasn't I with you at the time?' With a different pronoun it is easy enough: 'Aren't we all going together?' At a more elevated style level it is easy enough: 'Am I not going with you?' At a substandard style level it is easy enough: 'Ain't I going with you?' But at the precise place—stylistically, and with the stated subject, verb, and tense—described above, there is a hole in the pattern. There is no ordinary colloquial contraction of verb-form 'am' and negative element 'not'. The only one ever used besides 'ain't' is 'aren't', and 'Aren't I going with you?' is either pseudo-elevated or vulgar, not ordinary colloquial speech. The only thing for a speaker to do when the need to ask such a question arises is to ask some slightly different question instead: 'I thought I was going with you; isn't that right?'

14. One does not expect matching from language to language in this connection. It would be surprising if Chinese had this particular hole, or even grammatical patterns so similar that a closely comparable hole would be possible. But Chinese has its own holes. For example, it is difficult to distinguish between 'We all read those books' and 'We read all those books.' The 'all' is expressed with an adverb *dōu,* which grammatical habits require to be placed directly before the verb or separated therefrom only by one or more other adverbs. This adverb collectivizes a plurality itemized earlier in the sentence or in some previous utterance. 'I read all those books' is *nèisyē shū wǒ dōu nyàn le,* where *nèisyē shū* 'those books' comes at the beginning of the sentence and is collectivized by the *dōu.* 'We all read that book' is *nèibĕn shū wǒmen dōu nyàn le,* where *wǒmen* 'we' precedes and is collectivized by *dōu.* The sentence *nèisyē shū wǒmen dōu nyàn le,* where *dōu* is preceded by two substantive expressions which might be collectivized by it, means indifferently 'We all read those books', 'We read all those books', or even 'We all read all those books'.

15. Needless to say, fluent speakers of a language find their way around such holes without falling in. But even native speakers of a language can be inept, and a list of the pattern holes in a language is a good index of what specific ineptnesses will appear in the speech of a native speaker who has poor control of his language.

16. SUBJECT OF STUDY AND THE STUDY OF THE SUBJECT. Once the writer said to a chemist: "After all, all of chemistry can be regarded as a part of human history." His reply was "No; all of human history can be regarded as a part of chemistry." Both statements were potentially true, since the word 'chemistry' was being used in two different senses. In the first statement, the word meant 'the study of a particular range of phenomena'; in the second, it meant 'a particular range of phenomena', whether studied or not.

17. In a few cases, including chemistry, this same ambiguity is possible in Chinese. In others, e.g., physics or geography, it is not: *wùlĭ* 'physics (as an object of study)': *wùlĭsywé* 'physics (as the study of an object)'; *dìlĭ* 'geography (as object)': *dìlĭsywé* 'geography (as study)'. The cases in which the ambiguity is possible are mainly new importations from the West: *hwàsywé* 'chemistry' (either sense); *shùsywé* 'mathematics' (either sense, for the modern Westernized field). In these cases, the importation of perhaps desirable features of

Western culture into China has been accompanied by the importation of a kind of terminological confusion from which Chinese had theretofore been largely free.

18. NUMBER. Most English substantives are subject to the obligatory distinction of singular versus plural; exceptions, such as 'sheep', 'deer', superficially resemble all Chinese nouns, for which there is no such obligatory category. Because of the prevalence of the contrast in English, such a sentence as 'If you take that road watch out for the deer' may leave us unsatisfied: does the speaker mean one deer or an unknown plurality? This dissatisfaction has even led some interpreters of English grammar to insist that 'deer' and 'sheep' have plurals just like other nouns, except that in these cases the plurals are made by "zero change"—an interpretation which renders the cited sentence grammatically ambiguous rather than just semantically so.

19. On this score English and Chinese do not differ as to what it is possible to specify, but as to what is relatively easy, or hard, to specify. To indicate a particular variety of substance or thing (for which a noun exists), without any implication whatsoever as to quantity, is easy in Chinese. In English it is accomplished in certain contexts with a generic singular ('Man wants but little here below'), in others by a generic plural ('Professors shouldn't do things like that'), but in still other contexts it is accomplished only quite awkwardly: 'That student or those students who arrives or arrive after the assigned time . . .' . Legal English shows many such awkwardnesses.

20. In English, on the other hand, it is easy to specify an indefinite plurality (that is, any number from two on up, but not just one). This is awkward in Chinese; expressions such as those equivalent vaguely to 'a few', 'many', and the like are of course otherwise matched in English, and cannot be counted as performing the specific semantic function of which we are speaking.

21. With its obligatory categories, certain nouns in English show fluctuation in the agreeing verb: 'My family is coming to see me'; 'Are your family all well?' The choice between agreement and nonagreement is semantically functional on the stylistic level; Chinese, lacking the number categories, is forced to make do with other devices, none of which exactly matches this one.

22. CHANNELS OF METONYMY FOR MOTION AND LOCUS. In English, and probably generally in Western languages, verbs of motion from one place to another are also freely used to express constant spatial locus of an object, or change of spatial relationship of parts of an object as in growth:

'fall':   'A man fell from the top of a building'; 'The land falls about ten feet behind the house'; 'The cake fell'.

'run':   'He ran around the lake'; 'The road runs around the lake'; 'They ran the road around the lake'.

'split':   'His lip (was) split in the fight'; 'The treetrunk splits into three large branches close to the ground'.

23. In Chinese, verbs which carry the central meaning of motion are not used in such extended senses. The few exceptions must be suspected of having developed under Western influence.

24. TAKING AND HOLDING. Here the situation seems to be reversed. In English, 'take', 'grab', 'snatch', 'pick (up)', 'lift', 'seize', and the like refer only to the event of passing from non-possession to possession of an object, while other verbs, such as 'carry', 'hold', 'guard'—a smaller number, less highly differentiated—refer to the state of possession. 'Take' is marginal, verging on 'carry'. The progressive construction with 'keep' underscores the difference: 'He kept taking candy from the bowl' is a repetitive in meaning, whereas 'He kept (on) holding the spoon' is continuous.

25. In Chinese, on the other hand, there are a large number of verbs which denote, in themselves, simply grasping or holding of an object in a particular way, with one or another body part or associated artefact: *nyē:* between the fleshy part behind the nails of thumb and forefinger; *jwā:* in fingers partly closed, palm downwards; and many others. Any of these can be used inceptively (*tā bǎ jēn nyēchilaile* 'He picked up the pin') or continuatively (*tā nyēje jēn jǎu syàn* 'Holding the pin between her fingers she looks for the thread'); the difference depends on other elements in the sentences.

26. BREAKING. We have many words in English for various kinds of breaking: 'shatter', 'crumble', 'tumble', 'crack', 'split', 'tear'. Many of these are used, however, mainly when especially called for, rather than whenever the opportunity presents itself. If a window has shattered to splinters, we will normally report—if the report is unemotional—simply 'The window broke' or 'The window was broken'. To say 'The window (was) shattered' either is more emotional or is in response to a request for further detail.

27. In Chinese the normal unemotional report of any such event will usually use a more specific verb, of the kind first listed above. Individually these do not exactly match the English words, as these examples show:

dwàn: transverse breaking into segments of a long thin object, e.g., a pencil or tree branch;

lyè: to split without coming apart, as of a pane of glass with one or two long cracks, or a board or a drying surface;

swèi: to shatter into many small pieces, no longer in place relative to each other, as a pane of glass or a dish;

pwò: to break into a number of relatively larger pieces, most of which still hang together, as a pane of glass through which a bullet has passed, taking one small piece of glass away and leaving radial cracks, or a skull which has received a hard blow;

tā: to crumble down, collapse, as an old wall or house;

jà: to burst or explode outwards, as a bomb or balloon.

28. The word *hwài* is broader: 'to be or get out of order', as a watch or other mechanism, or an egg or piece of meat which is too old to eat, or a chair which still looks intact but which is apt to collapse *(tā)* if one sits on it. But *hwài* is not a generic for the specific terms listed above. When the window breaks, the normal Chinese report cannot be completely general; it will use *lyè, pwò, swèi,* or *jà* as the facts require.

29. In this and the two immediately preceding sections the examples seem to be more along the line of Whorf's interest than were those first given. We may perhaps call the example about cities and walls a "zero-order" difference: this is the kind we expect to find between any two languages. The fruits-and-nuts instance deserves then to be called a "first-order" difference: the point in this example is not that the semantic ranges of two relatively concrete nouns differ in the two languages (which would be a zero-order difference) but rather that there is divergence in the coverage of more inclusive generic terms. And if this is justified, then the motion-and-locus example deserves to be called a difference of even higher order. We have in it a situation in which not just one form from each language, but a whole semantically defined family of forms from each, have similar types of metaphorical or metonymic extension in English but not in

Chinese. A higher-order difference, then, is establishable when a whole set of zero- or first-order differences seem to manifest parallelism. The writer does not wish, however, to push this sorting-out of orders of difference too far, nor for the reader to expect any great precision in it—the writer has no idea, for example, what the difference between a "second-order" difference and a "third-order" difference would be.

30. HANDLING TIME AND SPACE. Whorf made so much of the difference between Hopi and Standard Average European in this connection that it would be unfortunate not to examine other languages in the same connection. But the writer has only one comment to offer; the details need much more close analysis.

31. Whorf claims that we handle time like space, or like a thing, whereas the Hopi do not.

32. In a footnote in *Language* (24 [1948], 160), Fang-Kuei Li writes, "These two villages are only a few miles distant from each other, but there are already slight dialectal differences."

33. What concerns us is the use of the word 'already'. Conceivably this sentence was "thought out" purely in English, so that the 'already' introduces a real reference to time: the relevant connection is not the short spatial distance between the two villages, but an implied relatively short interval of time since all the speakers of both villages were in intimate contact. It seems more likely that 'already' is Chinese *yǐjing* or *jyòu;* that is, that 'already' was inserted in the English sentence because in many contexts it is equivalent to *yǐjing* or *jyòu,* though in this specific context it is not. In Chinese—if our exegesis is correct—the reference is not to time at all, but genuinely to space, to the relatively short spatial distance between the villages; but it is a reference to space *handled like time.*

34. Or, put a bit differently, one could say that here, as in some other contexts, the Chinese make use of the linguistic machinery which they have on hand primarily for discussing temporal sequence and separation, in extended senses which are alien to English. A Chinese will say *Jèijāng jwōdz bǐ nèijāng cháng sāntswèn.* 'This table than that long three-inches'—'This table is three inches longer than that'. On occasion one will hear *Jèijāng jwōdz cháng sāntswèn le* 'This table long three-inches (particle for new state)'—'This table is three inches too long'. In the second one has, again, the use of a fundamental temporal element (the particle *le*) in an extended sense. The most tempting explanation is to say that the speaker has been looking for a table of a certain length, and has been examining a series of tables to find an appropriate one, so that upon examining the particular one on which the sentence comments, there has actually been a temporal sequence of events: the *le* means not that the table under discussion has changed its length, but that we, in looking at successive ones, have now arrived at one which is three inches too long. But this explanation is English, not Chinese; the writer fears that it is not really relevant. The safest statement we can make would probably be that in Chinese there is machinery used with reference to a variety of sequences and processes, some of which coincide with what we take as temporal. When the specific reference is temporal, the usage strikes us as normal; when it is not, it strikes us as alien.

35. Pigeonholes and Scales. Chinese verbs include a subclass which are "stative" and "intransitive," which for simplicity we can call adjectives. Individually, Chinese adjectives have meanings much like those of English adjectives: big, small, tall, short, and so forth. Many, but not all, are paired: *dà* and *syău* 'large, small'; *gāu*, and *ăi* 'tall, short'; *gāu* and *dī* 'high, low'; *cháng* and *dwăn* 'long, short'. This pairing is not just semantic; it is also shown structurally. In each pair, one member is the "major" member; this is shown by the selection of that member, rather than the other, in asking a colorless question about the degree of the particular quality. For example, just as in English, the normal question is 'How tall *(gāu)* is that building?'—and such a question as 'How short *(ăi)* is that building?' is most unusual.

36. Theoretically one can produce a grammatically complete sentence in Chinese by using a single substantive as subject and a bare adjective as predicate: *tā ăi* 'He's short.' In practice such sentences occur only in response to questions of the form *tā ăi buăi?* 'Is he (relatively) short or not?' In making de novo statements, a predicate which includes a stative verb invariably also has modifiers—the negative modifier *bù* 'not', or some indication of degree like *hěn* 'quite', *dzwèi* 'very', *jēn* 'really'.

37. This last is the most frequent style of adjectival predicate. We may say that a pair of Chinese adjectives establishes a scale, and specifies one direction on that scale as "positive." The normal adjectival predicate then serves to locate the subject somewhere along that scale, but always more or less relatively to other items, never in an absolute way. That is, Chinese adjectives most normally handle qualities overtly as matters of degree of difference, rather than as matters of kind (pigeonhole).

38. A point of departure for the relative judgment of some given object can be supplied using the coverb *bǐ* 'as compared with': *Jèijāng jwōdz bǐ nèijāng cháng* 'This table is longer than that one.' The relative judgment can then be rendered quantitative by using, after the stative verb, a combination of numeral and measure: *Jèijāng jwōdz bǐ nèijāng cháng sāntswèn* 'This table is three inches longer than that one.' If the *bǐ* phrase is omitted, this becomes, as already stated in the preceding section, a judgment of amount of undesirable excess: 'This table is three inches too long'. A different pattern states the length (or other quality) of an object in terms of metric units, which are of course overtly relative: *Jèijāng jwōdz yǒu sānchr cháng* 'This table is three feet long'. These are the various possible modifications of the essentially relativistic use of stative verbs.

39. There is also a pigeonhole pattern; one adds *de* to the adjectival predicate, nominalizing it so that it names a class or pigeonhole, and the statement asserts the membership of the subject in that class: *Nèijāng jwōdz (shr) chángde* 'That table is one of the long ones' or '. . . is a long one'. Such a statement, with this particular adjective, is made only in a context where some preceding act or speech has set up the classifications in question.

40. A few Chinese adjectives are used, in the predicate, only in this pigeonholing manner: *nán* and *nyǔ* 'male, female', for humans; *gūng* and *mǔ* 'male, female' for animals. Thus 'male' and 'female' are never matters of degree or relativity in Chinese; they are absolute pigeonholes. A few other adjectives tend to be used in this pigeonholing way at least as often as they are used in the relativistic patterns, if not somewhat more often: the five adjectives for the five fundamental tastes 'sweet', 'bitter', 'salty', 'sour', and 'peppery-hot'; perhaps color adjectives. Except for 'male' and 'female', adjectives which are structurally paired are used normally in the relativistic patterns, in the pigeonholing pattern only when special contexts render such usage appropriate.

41. Now we may ask whether there is any attribute of Chinese culture with which this habitual relativism correlates. It will be recalled that the Chinese "philosophy of life," as often reported from observation and as codified in some of the Chinese philosophico-religious systems, particularly Taoism, emphasizes a "doctrine of the mean": never get too happy, or you may also become too sad; moderation in all things. The writer does not know certainly that the speech-habit outlined above is an old one; literary Chinese is so divergent that judgment would be precarious if built on it, and what is needed is extensive dialect comparison. If the speech-habit is indeed old, then there may very well be a correlation between the speech-habit and the "philosophy of life."

42. This suggestion is put forward with great hesitation. There are several crucial problems in addition to the one already mentioned. For one, if there is indeed a determinable correlation, then it would impress the writer that the direction of causality in the matter is in all probability from "philosophy of life" to language, rather than vice versa—though, of course, the linguistic habit might serve as one of the mechanisms by which the philosophical orientation maintains its existence down through the generations. Even more disturbing is the possibility that careful examination of the use of adjectives in English and other Western languages might reveal that we have much the same semantic pattern as has been described above for Chinese. If so, then what becomes of our pretty hypothesis? We would have a similar linguistic pattern in Chinese and in the West; in Chinese it would be hooked up with a philosophy of life, but in the West it obviously would not.

43. SUMMARY. From a tentative discussion one can draw only tentative conclusions. Yet the following three generalizations seem to be reasonably well supported in the specific case of Chinese versus English. The writer feels that they probably hold for languages in general, and they have been phrased accordingly.

1. The most precisely definable differences between languages are also the most trivial from the Whorfian point of view. The more important an ostensible difference is from this point of view, the harder it is to pin down.

2. Languages differ not so much as to what *can* be said in them, but rather as to what it is *relatively easy* to say. In this connection it is worthy of note that the history of Western logic and science, from Aristotle down, constitutes not so much the story of scholars hemmed in and misled by the nature of their specific languages as the story of a long and successful struggle against inherited linguistic limitations. From the time when science became observational and experimental

this is easy to see: speech-habits were revised to fit observed facts, and where everyday language would not serve, special sub-systems (mathematics) were devised. But even Aristotle's development of the syllogism represented a sort of semantic purification of everyday Greek.

3. The impact of inherited linguistic pattern on activities is, in general, least important in the most practical contexts, and most important in such goings-on as story-telling, religion, and philosophizing—which consist largely or exclusively of talking anyway. Scientific discourse can be carried on in any language the speakers of which have become participants in the world of science, and other languages can become properly modified with little trouble; some types of literature, on the other hand, are largely impervious to translation.

Troubles of a different kind arise from gaps in languages which cannot be filled in translating because for a word that may be quite familiar in one language there is no equivalent in another. Probably the first example that will occur to many is the failure of French to provide a word for home. 'I shall go home', says the Englishman; and the Frenchman, *J'irai chez moi.* 'This is my home', says the Englishman on arrival; but the Frenchman can get no nearer than *Voilà ma maison,* or *mon logis* or *ma demeure* —all words whose primary significance is that contained in the English 'house' or 'residence'.

So, too, there is no English word for the French *menu,* or for the Latin word *augur;* there is no Latin for the English word 'premier'; and, admirable example, no Spanish word for 'jungle'. When Rudyard Kipling's *Jungle Book* was translated into Spanish its title became *El Libro de las Tierras Virgines.*

This kind of difficulty is frequent in the translation of all kinds of writings where the two nations whose languages are concerned may have different customs, different games and amusements, and different degrees of technical development. The habit of five-o'clock tea, for example, was introduced by the English to the French, whose language had no name for such a meal. It accordingly became known as *le fiveocloque,* and this gave rise to a corresponding verb, so that at one time one might read in a hotel the information that 'On *fiveocloque à quatre heures*'.

Theodore Savory,

*The Art of Translation**

*Reprinted by permission of Jonathon Cape, Ltd.

A given pattern is only obvious to certain categories of people. A man sees one thing in a room, a woman something else, a maid something else. This means there is a relationship between the people and patterns. In effect, groups can be defined by the relation of their members to a certain pattern. The individuals of a group share patterns that enable them to see the same thing and this holds them together.

Edward Hall,

*The Silent Language**

In the following essay Friedrich Waismann rebuts the doctrine of "the ordinary use of language" held by some philosophers and rhetoricians. His argument touches on points raised in other essays in this collection and bears particularly on a neglected implication of Whorf's hypotheses. If language habits determine and thus LIMIT the ways we think, then new and uncommon uses of language are also likely to lead to new and uncommon ways of thinking. Doctrines of "correct usage" among rhetoricians and of "stock use" among linguistic philosophers may be detrimental in poetry, science, and philosophy.

In Defense of New and
Uncommon Uses of Language

Friedrich Waismann

Language is always changing. That is a commonplace, yet, oddly enough, one not enough heeded by those who are clamouring for "the ordinary use of language", quite prepared, it seems, to damn everything out of hand—in philosophy—if it fails to conform to its standards. While appreciating the service done to clear thinking by the insistence on the normal use, I feel that the time has come to say a

From *Analysis*, Vol. XIII, No. 1 (October, 1952), copyright 1952, by permission of Basil Blackwell and Mott, Ltd.

word of warning against the cult of it, for such it has almost become. Like any cult, while it is likely to protect its votaries from certain dangers—getting trapped in the vagaries of speech—it is apt to make them blind to the obvious narrowness of such a view, particularly when it is just on the point of becoming one of the major influences of our time. It tends to instil, in the faithful and in the not-so-faithful alike, a belief, a complacent one, in the adequacy of language which is far from the truth. In actual fact, language is a deficient instrument, and treacherous in many ways. As this opens a subject of vast dimensions I shall confine myself to a few scattered observations.

2. First, I shall try to argue that a departure from the beaten track need not only not be anathematized, but may be the *very thing* to be strived for—in poetry, science and in philosophy. My second point is that language, far from serving merely to report facts, is a collective instrument of thought that enters experience itself, shaping and moulding the whole apprehension of phenomena (such as colour and lustre, e.g.) in a certain definite way, and, who knows, giving to them just that subtle bias which makes all the difference. How curiously different, for instance, must the world of colour have appeared to the Romans who had in their language no word for grey, brown, nor any *generic* word for blue (though they had a number of words to denote particular shades of this colour.) How curiously different, it would seem, must human action appear when seen through the filter of Eskimo language where, owing to the lack of transitive verbs, it is likely to be perceived as a sort of happening without an active element in it. (In Greenlandic one cannot say, 'I kill him', 'I shoot the arrow', but only 'He dies to me', 'The arrow is flying away from me', just as 'I hear' is expressed by 'me-sound-is'). Eskimo philosophers, if there were any, would be likely to say that what we call action is "really" a pattern, or gestalt, of succeeding impressions. Just as Greenlandic assimilates action to impression—which strikes us as strange—so our language tends to bias us in just the opposite way: it makes us assimilate perception to action. We say not only 'I cut the tree', but also 'I see the tree': the use of the same construction makes it appear as if the 'I' was the *subject* from which issued the seeing, and as if the seeing was a sort of action directed at the tree; nor are we any better off if we use the passive voice 'The tree is seen by me'—for now it almost looks as if something *happened* to the tree, as if it had to undergo or suffer my seeing it. Following the clues of speech, we are led

to interpret the world of experience one-sidedly, just as "owing to the common philosophy of grammar", as Nietzsche put it, i.e. "owing to the unconscious domination and guidance of similar grammatical functions the way seems barred against certain other possibilities of world-interpretation". In other words, every language contains, deep-sunken in it, certain moulds, designs, forms to apprehend phenomena, human action, etc. It is hardly going too far to say that a whole world picture is wedded to the use of the transitive verb and the actor-action scheme that goes with it—that if we spoke a different language we would perceive a different world. By growing up in a certain language, by thinking in its semantic and syntactical grooves, we acquire a certain more or less uniform outlook on the world—an outlook we are scarcely aware of until (say) by coming across a language of a totally different structure we are shocked into seeing the oddity of the obvious, or what seemed to be obvious. Finally, I want to say that philosophy *begins* with distrusting language—that medium that pervades, and warps, our very thought. But this is perhaps too strong an expression. I do not mean to say that language *falsifies* experience, twists it into something else; the point is that it supplies us with certain categorial forms without which the formation of a coherent system of experience, a world picture, would be impossible. In this sense, language shapes and fashions the frame in which experience is set, and different languages achieve this in different ways. A philosopher, more than others, should be sensitive to this sort of influence, alive to the dangers that lie dormant in the forms of expression—the very thing, that is, which, so misguidedly, has been raised to the standard in philosophical controversy.

When I spoke of the change of language I was not thinking of those cases which delight the heart of a philologist—umlaut, ablaut, and the like. Nor was I referring to changes in meaning and vocabulary—what was originally stupid, wanton, Latin *nescius*, becomes 'nice'; a horse that is well-fed and grows a smooth, shiny coat is 'glad'—*glatt* in German; what is now silly was formerly 'sely' corresponding to German *selig*—happy, blessed; for while such changes are instructive in many ways, they are hardly such as to deserve the philosopher's attention. Neither was I thinking of those more subtle changes in the *valeurs* of a word which—as in the case of 'romantic,—are significant of a change in the tone of thought of a whole period—of a half-conscious awakening of new ways of feeling and responses to nature, so elusive and yet, to the historian, so important. What I had in mind were cases which are best illustrated by a few examples.

3. Nothing is so opposed as day and night; yet there is a sense, as when we speak of a 'three days' journey', in which 'day' includes night. 'Man' is used in contrast to woman, but occasionally as a term including woman; and a similar shift of sense is perceptible in 'he' and 'she' —as an arguer, also woman is 'he'. We say of a child that he is two years 'old', not two years 'young', just as we inquire 'How *long* (not how *short*) will you stay?' or 'How *far* (not how *near*) is it from here to the station'? The word 'quality', while for the most part used indifferently, is sometimes uttered in a peculiar tone—as when we say 'He has quality'. White and black are commonly contrasted with colours in the strict and proper sense ('illustrations in colour' *versus* 'illustrations in black and white'), yet in certain contexts we are inclined to reckon them amongst the colours; as when we say 'Look round you— everything you see has some colour or other', thinking, perhaps, that even air and vapour, or glass and water are possessed by some very pale, some very pearly tone. Thus 'colour' tends to absorb into its meaning all shades, even black and white, the otherwise 'colourless' hues. But these are instances betraying a deeper drift. In the ordinary sense, motion is opposed to rest, speed to slowness, size to littleness, numerous to a few, depth to shallowness, strength to weakness, value to worthlessness, just as far is opposed to near, hot to cold, dry to wet, dark to bright, heavy to light, and true to false. And this was, roughly, the way in which Greek philosophers regarded such contrasts. 'Up' for them was simply 'not-down', 'soft' 'not-hard', 'dry' 'not wet', and so on. The fact that two polar terms were in use may have played a role in underpinning the belief that things which are hot and cold, or hard and soft, etc., are different, not in degree, but in kind—a fateful belief, for on it hinged their understanding—no, their lack of understanding of change. They signally failed to penetrate it. The Greeks never mastered the problem of motion—which is but the simplest case— they never evolved a science of dynamics, which is surprising enough in view of their genius for mathematics. They give the impression that they somehow got started on the wrong track—for them heavenly and terrestrial motion were entirely different, the one governed by law, eternal and unchanging, the other lawless, corrupt, confused; if faced with a change, such as a thing getting heated, they thought that one quality must be destroyed to let the opposite quality take its

place. Thus they were, perhaps as a consequence of their quaint ideas, mightily impeded in coming to grips with the problem of change.

4. In science a language has come into use in which those contrasted terms are looked upon as degrees of one and the same quality—darkness as light intensity of illumination, slowness as the lower range of speed, rest as the limiting case of motion; there is a scale only of hardness, not of softness, only a physical theory of heat, not a theory of coldness; what we measure is the strength of a rope, a current, etc., not its weakness, what we count is number, not fewness; the air has a degree of moisture, not of dryness; and everything has weight and mass, even an electron. Again, we speak of health irrespective of whether it is good or bad health, and of the value of things which are of no value. Under the influence of such examples, it would seem, a term like 'truth-value' has been coined to cover both truth and falsity of a statement, just as 'verification' is, prevalently, used to include falsification. 'Distance', 'width', 'wealth', 'intelligence' are further nouns which had the same career; though the same is not so true of the adjectives—'distant', 'wealthy', 'intelligent' are not yet relativized, any more than 'hard', 'hot', 'speedy', 'weighty' are, or 'healthy', 'valuable' and 'worthy'; on the contrary, they retain the original sense. Adjectives, it would appear, have a much tougher life than nouns, and not only in English. But that only in passing.

5. Here we see a whole array of terms shifting in a parallel way, and in a way which is of far-reaching consequence: for the construction of modern science is bound up with it and would not have been possible without it. The change-over from the static view—where the adjective is seen as the expression of a permanent quality—to a dynamical which apprehends quality as a variable degree within a certain scale made possible 'functional thinking' (I use the word as mathematicians do), the kind of thinking that can cope with change and the conceptual difficulties it presents. What happened was obviously this: one term of a pair of contraries had a tendency to swallow up the other and stand for the whole range of variation. Whether this tendency can be traced to the rationalising influence of science, or whether it is prior to science and has itself given us impetus to that revolution of thought is a question still undecided. It is in this context, perhaps, not without significance that Latin and Greek were lacking in all the finer means to express continuous change and functional dependence: in Latin, for instance, there are no *general* terms to express the relation "the more—the less"; the phrases used for "the more—the more" are confined to simple *proportionality*, the analogue to *statics*. Nor has any classical language an equivalent for 'to become' (*devenir* in French, *devenire* in medieval Latin) so essential to our way of describing a change in quality, for neither *fieri* nor γίγνεσθαι can be used in the same way to express the idea of *continuous* change. There are no uses of intransitive verbs such as 'to soften', (*rubesco* is inceptive), etc.

6. The new idiom, which sprang up first in the vernacular about the 14th century, has not entirely displaced the older one (as can still be seen from the adjectives cited above). Both exist side by side. Though the use of 'moisture' for dry as well as wet (as in meteorology), or of 'truth-value' in logic still has the ring of jargon, in other instances the new idiom has become completely naturalised—as with 'distance' for near and far, 'age' for young and old, 'size' for big and small, 'density' for thick and thin. Yet even so, we can use any such term in two distinct ways—we may ask '*Is* he old?' or '*How* old is he?'; and so in the other cases.

7. At the time of Nicole Oresme, Bishop of Lisieux, when a new way of looking at change was growing up, and with it a new way of speaking of qualities, this must have been felt as a shocking departure from the ordinary use, supported and sanctioned as it was by old tradition. How the cloisters of the schoolmen must have resounded with 'intensio et remissio formarum'—the disputes as to whether a quality might have degrees and, in changing, could yet remain the same, or whether this was patent nonsense. One may imagine the indignant outcries of the purists of the time, their loathing of what must have appeared to them as "new-fangled ways of speaking" and as a "complete perversion" of grammar. The latter, more even than the vocabulary, embodies a good deal of the conservatism of mankind, and progress had often to be made in the teeth of the enormous resistance offered by its structure to ways of thinking which do not, or not smoothly, fit its grooves. (See what has been said in the foregoing on Greek language and absence of dynamics.) Grammar draws a *cordon sanitaire* against any rebellious ideas that dare to crop up.

8. The importance of functional correlation can, moreover, be seen in a different domain: in perspective, and the enthusiasm with which it was universally greeted when it was discovered—another coincidence?—at the very time when new aspects of thought and feeling were just about to take shape: Duccio's Maesta and Giotto's wall paintings in the Capella degli Scrovegni in Padua both belong to the early 14th century. The "strange fascination which perspective had for the Renaissance mind cannot be accounted for exclusively by a craving for verisimilitude", as Panofsky observes. A sensibility to functional relation is apparent in this, and the interest in perspective—so alien to the Greeks—is almost symbolic of the time. A reflex of it can still be caught from the writings of Leonardo da Vinci and Dürer. As perspective rests essentially on a clear understanding of the way in which two variables, the apparent size of an object and its distance from the beholder, are connected, Leonardo saw in painting a 'science'. He certainly must have been struck by the affinity between this 'science' and the philosophical speculations on dynamics of the schoolmen of which he was fully aware (he even employed their ideas in his theory of painting).

9. If those pedantic schoolmen and-masters had had their way, there would to-day be no science and no dynamics; but, for consolation, 'correct' grammar. To look at any departure from the norm as a crime is nothing but a blind prejudice; and a fateful one at that as it tends to drain the life-blood of any independent inquiry. Language is an instrument that must, as occasion requires, be bent to one's purpose. To stick to language as it is can only lead to a sort of Philistinism which insists on the observance of the *cliché* and will end up with a harakiri of living thought. Indeed, the guardian of language who jealously watches over its 'correctness' is in the long run bound to turn into a reactionary who looks askance at any innovation. Correctness is a useful, but a negative virtue. Follow those prophets, and you will soon find yourself imprisoned in a language cage, clean, disinfected, and unpleasant like a sanatorium room.

10. Understandably enough, there is an instinctive prejudice against neologisms, in part springing from a wholesome fear that novelty of speech may screen poverty of thought. We all dislike new words. And yet there is another and perfectly proper urge to give expression to meanings so far unexpressed, or, in the present language, indeed inexpressible. When Freud, for instance, says *der Patient erinnert den Vorfall* he is using the verb *erinnern* in a novel manner; in the ordinary way, the verb is used reflexively, *sich an etwas erinnern*. Why has Freud (who wrote a very good style) diverged at this point? There is a queer way in which a neurotic person who is under treatment may suddenly remember long-forgotten scenes of his early life which, as Freud puts it, have been 'repressed' and are now being re-lived. What has been inaccessible to the patient, however hard he may have tried, breaks, in a violent storm of emotion, through to consciousness. In order to set apart this kind of remembrance from the ordinary one where we remember at will, Freud uses the verb transitively, in a way no one has done before; and with this syntactical innovation goes a semantic change. By this use Freud has enriched the German language. Such stray deviations, hit upon in a lucky hour and accepted by custom, these little, yet expressive departures from the beaten track, have not only a vividness, a sparkle of their own, but they sharpen the tools of thought and keep language from going blunt. So why cavil at them?

11. What those sticklers for correctness prefer not to see is that we are living in a *changing world,* and that language is always lagging behind these changes. To cite only one sort of examples out of a great many parallel ones—in psychological experiments one constantly comes across situations which call for new ways of describing. If Maxwell disks, for instance, are rotated one sees, so long as the movement is slow, several colour sectors, and when the disk is spinning rapidly, a uniform colour, the result of fusion, but in between there is a certain point where a flicker is seen. There are cases in which the colour itself is seen flickering, and others, as when the disk is watched through a small screen-hole, which are more aptly described by saying that there is a flickering *across* the disk or *before* it in space, or again that the disk's surface is seen *behind* the flicker. These modes of expression, though perfectly natural and instantly understood by every one, yet digress from the norm. For 'before' and 'behind', while clearly denoting spatial relations, are used in such a way that it makes no longer sense to ask, 'Exactly how many millimeters before the disk is the flickering? Here we have a sense of 'before' which admits of no distance. To cite a few similar cases—if we look at a metal its colour seems to lie *behind* its surface, just as its glitter appears *in front of,* or *superimposed* on it; the glow of a piece of red-hot iron is seen not simply as colour that lies on its surface but as *extending back* into the object. Again, it has been said that, when a person is speaking with someone in complete darkness, the voice of the other sounds distinctly *behind* the darkness, not *in* the darkness. In some cases an object is seen as 'desurfaced', with a filmy, fluffy sort of outline, a bit unreal

perhaps. Queer idioms which say what cannot quite be said by anything else: but condemn them on account of that? Notice with what
unerring instinct language contrives to say, at the cost of a slight departure, what would be unsayable if we moved along the rigid grooves
of speech. Indeed, how should one describe such phenomena if not
by breaking away from the *clichés*? Is there anything objectionable
in that? If so, language could never keep pace with life. Yet new situations, unforeseen, arise, and with them the need of describing them;
it can only be met by adjusting language—either by coining new
words, or, as the word-creating faculty is scanty, by pressing old ones
into new services, in this way cutting through the dead mass of convention. It is precisely because speech runs so much in ready-made
moulds that an occasional anomaly, a happy flouting of the laws of
grammar, an uncommon phrasing, arouses our attention and lends
lustre to the point we want to bring out. It is in this way, by *trans-
gressing*, that language manages to achieve what it is meant to
achieve, and that it grows. Why, then, the squeamishness?

12. Not only should the scientist be free to deviate from common
language, where the need arises, but he is bound to do so if he is to
convey a new insight not in conformity with the ideas dominant of
the time, with ideas, moreover, precipitated in language. The classical
example of this is Einstein. When he was groping his way, there was,
in his own words, 'a feeling of direction', of going towards something
he didn't quite know—which centred more and more on a suspicion
that all was not well with the idea of simultaneity. He could at first
not say what was wrong with it, and yet felt that here, if anywhere,
was the key to all the dark puzzles that troubled the physicists at that
time. Had he been brought up as a pupil of G. E. Moore, imbued with
a belief in the infallibility of the ordinary modes of expression, he
could never have made his discovery, clogged as he would have been
by the dead weight of usage. As it was, he paid no respect to common
sense, let alone the common speech. He insisted on asking himself,
Do I *really* understand what I mean when I say that two events are
simultaneous? Once the question was brought into sharp focus, he
came to see, gradually perhaps and to his surprise, that there was a
gap in his understanding. For the sense in which we speak of two
events happening at the same time, when they are in the same place,
or nearby, cannot be applied to events in distant places. It would be
blind, he felt, to apply the familiar meaning of 'simultaneous' to these

other cases—it would only land us in perplexities beyond resolve. Einstein saw that the term 'simultaneous' had first to be *defined* for the case of distant events, and defined in such a way that the definition supplies us with a method to decide experimentally whether or not two events are simultaneous. This 'seeing' of a crucial point in the meaning of 'simultaneous' has *absolutely nothing* to do with the way the word is actually used in language. It is as well to remind you that in 1905, when Einstein's first essay appeared, there was only *one* use, not two uses of 'simultaneous', and that it would be absurd to pretend that, when Einstein found a difference in meaning, he was making a *linguistic* discovery. (A side-light on how wrong the philosophical equation meaning = use is). On the contrary, anyone who had taken ordinary language, or common sense, for his guide, and had been asked whether he understood what 'simultaneous' meant, would have replied with a decided Yes—no matter whether he could, or could not, specify a method for finding out. He would have said that the meaning of the word is clear in itself and needs no further explanation. In fact, no one before Einstein, whether a plain man, a scientist, or a philosopher, doubted for a minute that the concept was clear to him, so clear that he need not trouble. That's precisely what made people slur over the decisive point. Einstein *saw*: that is how he freed himself from the thought-habits imposed on us by speech, radically so. By following the lead of language, or of the common sense philosophers one would have barred oneself from the spark of insight which was to be the dawn of a new era in physics.

13. These facts speak for themselves. That science cannot live under the tutelage of any ideas on 'correctness', will perhaps be conceded. But this is true not only of science. Poetry is forever groping along the borders of the unspeakable, wresting new land from the vast void of the unexpressed. It is its mission to break through the wall of conventional views that encloses us, to startle us into seeing the world through fresh eyes. This is what all the great poets from Dante to Baudelaire have performed, and that is their glory. However, it is a large subject, too large to be treated here. I shall pick out only one tiny point, and one, moreover, that concerns prose—Flaubert's style which, in Proust's phrase, has 'renewed our vision of things'. In a work of fiction, nature is usually treated as background to men; against this background stand out the main characters of the story, the way they act, think, speak, feel and behave. The contrast between the uniformity of nature and the uniqueness of the human world is, in French, expressed by the use of two tenses—the imperfect for things and processes, and the perfect for men and actions. But with Flaubert, what men do is, in essence, always the same—it is like the succession of rain and sunshine, spring and summer, the ripening of the corn, and the phases of the moon. There is something dull and re-petetive [sic] about them which pervades them with a sort of disapas-sionate sadness. There is a passage in *Madame Bovary* where Flaubert speaks of "the eternal monotony of passion which has ever the same forms and the same language". A revealing passage; for what he has tried to do and has done is to bring about something like a shift in our way of seeing people and things; and this he achieves, simply, by his relentless use of the imperfect, assimilating, in language, his apprehension of men to that of things, (remember Greenlandic!) Everything, including human action, is resolved into a perpetual and monotonous flux, revealing the melancholy essence of human exis-tence. Describing people in the forms appropriate to things produces a peculiar effect indeed—"what, up to the time of Flaubert, had been merely action, has become impression", as Proust puts it. As we read over the pages of his novels, we are made to feel in what people say that they would always say precisely the same thing, that their whole life can be poured into a phrase as into a little vial. And when the perfect is used—on rare occasions only as when the narrative changes direction—it is again with a queer effect: it gives to a thing (when it occupies the place of a subject) a character of activity, it is as if a furtive ray of sunlight was falling on it, imparting to it, for a fleeting instant, a life of its own: change suddenly turns into action. And from this arises that unique Flaubertian vision of things which, like any artist's vision, can only be communicated through his style. Besides the tenses, the conjunction 'and' is used in an entirely new way. It hardly ever binds phrase to phrase, but has a more musical function —to mark a pause in the beat of the rhythm, to indicate that the mov-ing wave we have been following has spent itself, and that another is about to build itself up. To this must be added a novel use of the pres-ent participles, of adverbs, and of certain pronouns and prepositions —grammatical peculiarities which all contribute to give shape to a world picture in which life is seen as a smooth change of one state passing into another without the persons taking any active part in the action—a picture that reminds one of some huge escalator which goes on and on, never stopping, never breaking its monotony. But where an 'action' does intervene in the flow of events, its protagonists are, in general, *things*, acting on a plane of nonhuman drama. What a vision! And yet a vision attained by distorting syntax. This, I think, should be enough to instil a drop of scepticism into the belief that all is well with ordinary language; it makes one wonder whether there is not, after all, a hard atom of truth in the view that ordinary speech is only good for saying things that are no longer worth saying.

14. By giving so copious examples my aim was to drive home the point defended here—that the ideal of correctness is a deadening one, that it is in vain to set up a language police to stem living developments. (I have always suspected that correctness is the last refuge of those who have nothing to say).

15. Poets and literary critics feel, today perhaps more keenly than ever before, that there is something disquieting about language. If I correctly read the signs, there is a susceptibility to the perils of words, a growing one, and a suspicion that language comes between us and the things we want to say. "In speaking one always says more than one intends to" observes Sartre; and T. S. Eliot, having noticed the vanity of words to express what is unique in experience, says "The particular has no language". Philosophers, on the other hand, are on the whole more likely to be found in the opposite camp—'debunking' all this talk as "pseudo-complaints which masquerade as genuine". I think that this is a mistaken attitude for a number of reasons, and this is perhaps the place to set out some of them.

16. First, to talk of *the* ordinary use of language is, as I have already hinted in a previous article, unrealistic. Though I would not go so far as Ezra Pound in saying that our whole speech is "churning and chugging" today, the fact remains that language is in a state of flux. But, it will be said, that is the concern of the historian of language, not of the philosopher. All the philosopher needs to know is the *stock*-use of a word or phrase, as it is employed at present, in contrast with its non-stock uses. This answer is unsatisfactory. Though it would be silly to pretend that one did not know the stock-use of 'cat' or 'shut the door', there are other cases where one would feel less sure. Is a 'taste of onions' the stock-use and a 'taste for history' derived, secondary, figurative? (But it is not *felt* as a metaphor!) Is only a 'brilliant sunshine' standard-use and a 'brilliant style' non-standard? Is 'day' as opposed to night, or as including night the norm? What about speaking of a 'wild laughter', a 'brooding silence', or saying that a 'recollection of this experience moved in his eyes'? It is easy to see that the 'stock-use' shifts with the context, and shifts in time. What was stock-use may become obsolescent and fall into the limbo of silence, just as new uses may spring up and may, in their turn, become standard language; but where is one to draw the line? It is well to remember that almost all expressions which refer to the mental are derived from others whose primary sense was sensuous and that this is a process which goes on to the present day; just as a good many words, under the influence of science, philosophy, or something still more elusive, have only in fairly recent times undergone a change in meaning—e.g. 'organic', 'nervous', 'unconscious', 'original', 'creative', 'objective', 'curiosity', 'to entail', etc. There is continuous change and continuous creation in language. Finally, there is such a thing as ambiguity which—except in exceptional cases—mars any attempt to single out one use as the stock one. Exactly how many standard-uses has 'nature'? What about 'in', 'on', 'about' etc.? "The English prepositions", says Empson, "from being used in so many ways and in combination with so many verbs, have acquired not so much a number of meanings as a body of meaning continuous in several dimensions." If so, or if the uses shade off into one another imperceptibly, how can one peel off and throw away all the non-stock uses and retain the stock ones? Yes, this view *is* unrealistic.

17. Next, and this raises a bigger issue, even if there was such a thing as a stock-use, it need not matter much to the philosopher. I mean, he need not be *bound* to this use; I should even go further and say that, sooner or later, he is bound to commit the crime and depart from it— that is, if he has something new to say. In this respect, his position is not altogether different from that of the poet or the scientist, and for similar reasons. He, too, may have come to see something which, in the ordinary way, cannot quite be said. I shall argue later that this is a characteristic feature of some philosophising. To mention here just one small point, the English language has been enriched by many words coined by philosophers who were sensitive to gaps in our vocabulary. 'Optimism', for instance, is due to Leibniz, and was borrowed from him by Voltaire. 'Impression' in its modern sense was introduced by Hume, 'intuition' by De Quincey, 'intuitionism' by Sidgwick, 'intuitionist' by H. Spencer. 'Scientist' is an invention of Whewell, 'aesthetic' one of Baumgarten, and so on. That even the

laws of grammar can be flouted with salubrious effect can be seen from Lichtenberg's remark that one should say 'It thinks in me'.

18. My third point is that certain features of one's own language are noticed and appreciated in their full significance only when it is compared with other languages—with German (verbal way of expressing colour), Greenlandic (dominance of the impression verb), Latin (absence of words for blue, grey, and brown), etc. Is, then, the philosopher to go to the Eskimos to learn his trade? Not exactly; yet the mere *awareness* of other possibilities is, philosophically, of the utmost importance: it makes us see in a flash other ways of world-interpretation of which we are unaware, and thus drives home what is conventional in our outlook. The technique of the ordinary-use philosophers has suffered from the fact that they restricted themselves to the study of one language to the exclusion of any other—with the result that they became blind to those ubiquitous features of their own language on which their whole mode of thinking, indeed their world picture, depends.

19. Connected with this is another large point—the misleadingness of our speech-forms. That language, "the embodied and articulated Spirit of the Race", as Coleridge put it, is in many ways inadequate can, I take it, by no one be doubted. In particular, it is the syntax and the field of analogies embedded in language which, unperceived, hold our thought in thrall, or push it along perilous lines. We shall soon have occasion to substantiate this point.

20. But there are still more reasons for guarding against this official doctrine. The one is that its champions pay heed only to the actual use of language not to its gaps revealing as they are. Suppose, for instance, that I say 'I ought to do so-and-so'; when I say that it is obvious that the I is here only a pseudo-subject from which the ought seems to proceed, whereas in fact it is more a *point d'appui* to which it is directed. We regard a rule of ethics, politeness, etc., as something outside ourselves which applies to us as objects. We are rather in a passive (obedient) frame of mind, and what is active is, at most, the consent we give to that duty. 'I am under an obligation,' 'it is my duty' are therefore phrases which are more appropriate. That 'ought' does not refer to an occult activity betrays itself in a number of features; thus we do not say 'I will ought', 'I choose (decide) to ought', any more than we say 'I ought to ought' or 'I am resolved upon oughting'. There is no such thing as a 'will to ought'. The complete absence of these idioms *is* revealing. That philosophers have concentrated on the use, and neglected the non-use of expressions is a further weakness of their technique.

21. But there is another and more serious danger lurking in this approach which is best expressed in a comparison. Just as Hume has tried to make association do the work for reason and failed, so a similar danger is involved in the teachings of Moore, and still more in that of his followers—in that they rely on the machinery of *language* to do the thinking for them, without exercising judgment. In both cases the mistake is to trust in something blind, mechanical, to ignore what is understanding, insight. Only this can explain such a monstrous utterance as that of N. Malcolm (approved by J. Wisdom) that one learns necessary truths by 'the eyes and the ears'—by attending, namely, to the way in which people use words. Surely, what we learn, and all we can learn in this way, are language *habits*. The story told is somewhat like this. A child watches on Monday two people speaking and the one of them saying 'A camel is larger than a flea'; on Tuesday he overhears the other chap saying 'A flea is smaller than a camel'; on Wednesday——. So after weeks of strenuous observation, checking and cross-checking, he arrives at the necessary truth that B is smaller than A follows from A is larger than B, and *vice versa*.

I find it recornered in my nosebook that it was a dokey and winnie dave towart the end of Marge in the ear of our Loaf 1892 in Much Bladder, a city off the North Wold. Shamrock Womlbs had receeded a telephart whilst we sat at our lunch eating. He made no remark but the matter ran down his head, for he stud in front of the fire with a thoughtfowl face, smirking his pile, and casting an occasional gland at the massage. Quite sydney without warping he turd upod me with a miscarriage twinkle in his isle.

"Ellifitzgerrald my dear Whopper," he grimmond then sharply "Guess whom has broken out of jail Whopper? My mind immediately recoughed all the caramels that had recently escaped or escaped from Wormy Scabs.

"Eric Morley?" I ventured. He shook his bed. "Oxo Whitney?" I queered, he knotted in the infirmary. "Rygo Hargraves?" I winston agreably.

"No, my dear Whopper, it's OXO WHITNEY" he bellowed as if I was in another room, and I wasn't.

"How d'you know Womlbs?" I whispered excretely.

"Harrybellafonte, my dear Whopper." At that precise morman

a tall rather angularce tall thin man knocked on the door. "By all accounts that must be he, Whopper." I marvelled at his acute osbert lancaster.

"How on urge do you know Womlbs" I asped, revealing my bad armchair.

"Eliphantitus my deaf Whopper" he baggage knocking out his pip on his large leather leg. In warped the favourite Oxo Whitney none the worse for worms.

John Lennon, "The SinguLARGE Experience

of Miss Anne Duffield," *A Spaniard in the Works*

Other essays in the present collection, particularly Whorf's and Ullmann's, have suggested that the language one speaks influences and partially determines one's view of reality. If this is so, what of speakers of dialects? Do they share a reality different from our own?

In "Mountain Speech," an edited version of two longer essays, Cratis Williams considers some features of the dialect of the Southern Mountains of the United States, and he suggests that in several ways it is a more poetic language than Standard English. Is it possible that Southern Mountaineers have a more "poetic" view of the universe than we do? Can we say that their language is somehow better or worse than ours?

Mountain Speech

Cratis Williams

Forming the rhythmic patterns of the speech of the people of the Southern Mountains are low intonations, leisurely pace and, in matters of grammar and diction, that lack of self-consciousness which precludes the false starts and sputterings sometimes heard in the speech of the educated.

Reprinted from *Mountain Life and Work*, XXXVII:3, Fall, 1961 (pp. 7-10) and XXXVIII:1, Spring, 1962 (pp. 15-19).

2. The use of ancient, strong past-tense forms of verbs, archaic sub-junctives, early English participles, old-fashioned prepositions, pleo-nasms (rifle-gun, boy-baby, hound-dog, etc.), and heavy stress on certain final syllables (presi*dent,* judg*ment*) produces metrical pat-terns similar to those found in traditional nursery rhymes, riddles, ballads, and folk songs. Contractions, elisions, and telescopings un-familiar to the ear of the cultured outsider, archaic tags, strange idioms, and involved prepositional clusters belonging to another day, elaborate negative constructions, localisms, and a strictly observed but unself-conscious traditional grammar produce a poetic quality similar to that of folk epics and the quaint reliques of primitive peo-ple.

3. The Southern Highlanders, along with Southerners generally, omit *g* in *ing* endings. Strictly speaking, the *g* is not omitted, of course, for it was never there in the first place. Passing by oral tradition through a series of generations of relatively unlettered folk, what appears today in cultured English as *ing* is in mountain speech the *un* (the vowel a schwa) to which the Anglo-Saxon participle ending *ende* was reduced in time. The absence of the palatal *ing,* which tends to put a brake on rhythm in cultured speech, facilitates the liquid flow of the moun-taineer's speech, and particularly so because the schwa ties the sylla-ble to the preceding one so closely that it invariably becomes the lightest kind of *unstress: a-com'n, a-fight'n, a-hoe'n,* etc. This charac-teristic of the mountaineer's use of the *ing* ending differentiates it from that of other Southerners, who tend to syllabicate *in'* more strongly, as in *com-in, writ-in, help-in,* and who sound the vowel short as in *tin.*

4. The Middle English preposition *a* (usually meaning *on, in, by*), the indefinite article *a* (never *an!*), the idiomatic use of *a* with *all* and numbers (as Chaucer used it) serve as cushions in keeping mountain speech flowing smoothly. The unstressed prefix *be-* (pronounced *bĭ-*), the spurious schwa inserted in polysyllabic words, the syllabic endings of certain plural nouns and singular verbs in the third person of the present tense, the fondness for such adjectival inflections as *-y, -ish, -ācious,* and *-like* lend a melodic quality to the mountaineer's speech which may be unique in modern times.

5. Certain traditional rules of grammar enhance the melody of the highlander's speech. It is noteworthy in this regard that *m* is more melodic than *s* and more easily managed than *z. Them* as a demonstrative adjective is universally used, frequently by the college bred, in preference to those, a word to which the mountaineer is instinctively averse. *Yourn, hisn, hern, ourn, theirn (your one, your own,* etc.), and *youns* or *younse,* as well as *thisn* and *thatn,* possess a musical quality of their own. The use of *hisself* and *theirself* or *theirselves* (pronounced *hisse'f,* etc.) in preference to *himself* and *themselves* is perhaps the same expression of the enormous respect for the integrity of *self* as that reflected in political and religious writings of the eighteenth century, for *his own self* and *their own selves* are frequently heard. Eschewing the use of such contractions as *isn't, aren't, hasn't, haven't,* and *hadn't* (for which *ain't* or *hain't,* as the rhythm and emphasis require, is quite generally substituted), the mountain man trips lightly over many a phrase with which the tongue of his better-favored contemporary would labor awkwardly. The relative pronoun *that* does triple service for the highlander, for *who* and *which,* although occurring frequently as interrogatives, are simply not used as relative pronouns. Moreover, *what* as a relative pronoun referring to persons, although sometimes placed in the mouths of mountain folk by novelists, is practically unknown in the entire mountain region.

6. Mountain people become dramatic easily. In moments of excitement and anger they rise to superb heights in the quality of their rhetoric. In reciting personal experiences or telling what they have been witness to they display qualities which belong to the best of oral literature. They love figures of speech, trenchant epigrams, compound oaths, and superlative phrases, but at the same time they have scrupulous regard for the exact detail and the actual fact. Even the most illiterate mountain folk are familiar with the contents of the King James Version of the Bible, frequently through oral tradition, and Biblical quotations find their way easily into mountain speech. Rhetorical devices of Elizabethan prose, even to exaggerated scurrility, may be identified by the careful listener.

7. Following are illustrations of mountain speech:

To the dog: Begone! Git out'n hyar, you torn-down critter, afore I break ever' bone *in* ye with this hyar arn poker! *(Turning to the guest.)* Now, watch *at* it! Hit won't be five minutes 'till that bag o' fleas'll be right back in hyar a-swarpin' an' a-swarvin' around. Ye can drive it out a dozen times, an' airy time ye have a mind to look ye can see the lowdown thang a-layin' on the hath-rock a-snappin' at its fleas and a-smoulin' over hitself. *(Spitting toward the fireplace.)* Sometimes I wish, by ____, ever' dog on this hyar place was right in the fur fork of hell with its backbroke. They hain't a one on the place, an' I reckon we got a dozen of 'em, that's wuth the powder and lead hit'd take to blow its brains out. Let a chicken git in the gyarden, an' ye can bawl yer head off fer a dog, but won't nary one on the place come a-nigh ye.

8. *Farmer to a passer-by:* Horry! Wull, sur, she's a hot'n, hain't she? Sixty-two degrees hotter'n hell, I reckon. I've been a-settin' hyar under the shade o' this hyar mulbarry bursh the pa-ast ha-alf a ăuer, an' 'pyears like I cain't git a *breath* o' frash air. I'm a-dreddin' them weeds like pizen, too. Agin I got my crap hoed out'n the fust weeds, the tides come. Hit's been so wet a body couldn't afford to rurn his ground a-workin' it, and the weeds a-gittin' vagrouser an' vagrouser ever' day. Withouten ye git yer crap hoed out afore the June tides come, ye just might as well fer to set down an' set thar, looks like. Try to work an' ye cain't do no good no how don't 'pyear like, in this hyar heat hotter'n the middle kittle of hell. Why don't ye light an' let yer saddle rest? We'll go out to the hăuse atter 'while and let ye see how pore folks live. The ole womern come out an' holp me a little while, but she's down thar now a-whackin' off chunks o' hog's jowl as big as yer hand and' a-throwin' 'em in the pot o' leather-britchy beans. They'll be larrupin' good fer sartain shore agin ye can step on the head o' yer shadder.

9. Mountain speech at the folk level probably differs little from the common speech of the semiliterate masses living on the American frontiers during the eighteenth and early nineteenth centuries. Transscriptions of present-day mountain speech written out reveal only slight differences from vernacular American English placed in the mouths of backwoodsmen in the 1830's by such writers of fiction as James Hall and John Pendleton Kennedy. Southern humorists recorded the same general kind of speech. When written down, contemporary mountain speech brings back memories to Midwesterners of ancient grandfathers and lusty companions swapping yarns around pot-bellied stoves in crossroads stores.

II

10. The primitive strength of mountaineer speech is exerted largely in verbs and the spare economy with which they function in the communication of ideas. Five of the most common verbs ordinarily retain their infinitive forms throughout the tenses. Only contextual use, for example, would reveal the tense of *begin, come, eat, give, run*. That trey of troublesome verb pairs, *lie-lay, rise-raise, sit-set*, which presents perennial problems to so many teachers of English is of no concern whatever to the highlander, who not only consistently uses *lay, laid, laid* and *set, set, set* both transitively and intransitively but who would under no circumstances be guilty of using *lie* and *sit*. If he is an old timer, he might say *rise, riz, riz*, but if he is the more common type of mountaineer he uses *raise, raised, raised* in intransitive constructions. Other common verbs have the same form in both the past and the perfect tenses: *do, done, done; go, went, went; know, knowed, knowed; see, saw, saw* (sometimes, *see, seed, seed*); *sing, sung, sung; take, tuck, tuck; ride, rode, rode* (or *ride, rid, rid*); and *write, wrote, wrote* (or *write, writ, writ*). This habit of leveling a verb to one or two tense forms increases the facility of the verb and tends to enhance the rhythmical quality of speech.

11. Prejudiced preferences for the foregoing verb forms is unaccountably strong in the mountaineer. The average child from the mountain home, unwilling to subject himself to the blistering sarcasm of his elders, clings to the local forms even when he knows the modern forms, for the condemnation that one is "gittin' above his raisin'," or "up-headed," or "stuck up," or "too big for his britches" carries terrible implications among people whose highest accolade for the returned migrant is that he is still "as common as a old shoe-rag," "you cain't tell no difference in 'im," "he's jest the same as ever," or "he's jest the same old Rafe."

12. Certain prejudices in the use of the verb *be* obtain as well. *Were* is normally used *only* in subjunctive constructions: when I *were* a boy, hit *were* a shame, etc. *Was* is used for both singular and plural in the indicative mood. Sometimes a present subjunctive is substituted for what would normally be a past form: if I *be* you. Much use is made of present subjunctive, however: if it *be* so. *Isn't, aren't, hasn't, haven't* are strictly avoided. *Ain't* or *hain't*, depending on the need for emphasis, is used universally in the place of these "furrin" contractions. The bright mountain boy eager to improve his English but determined to avoid the use of *ain't* is constrained to use *he's not* and *they've not* in lieu of *he isn't* and *they haven't* if he wishes to escape the damnatory label of being "stuck up."

13. Writers of fiction have been most impressed with those verbs which retain either the strong preterites of Middle English or variant preterites of the English dialects. It is perhaps these verbs that most readily attract the attention of outsiders to the peculiarities of mountain usage. Not unusual in English dialects, they are impressive solely because of their frequency. Following are some of the most common of these verbs:

Present	Past	Past Participle
ax	axt	axt
bring	brung	brung
climb	clim	clim
	clomb	clomb
	clumb	clumb
catch	cotch	cotch
dreen	dreened	dreened
	drint	drint
drive	driv	driv
drap	drapt	drapt
fetch	fotch	fotch
fight	fit	fit
freeze	friz	friz
heat	het	het
help	holp	holp
hold	helt	helt
	hilt	hilt
leap	lope	lope
light	lit	lit
rake	ruck	ruck
reach	rech	rech
send	sont	sont
skin	skun	skun
slide	slid	slid
	slud	slud
sneak	snuk	snuk
wrop	wropt	wropt

14. Mountain people consistently avoid the use of past tense forms in which *a* or *ew* in general English usage is substituted for some other vowel appearing in the infinitive form. Not only are *began, came, ate, gave,* and *ran* not used, but *drank, rang, sang, sank,* and *swam* are avoided as well. *Blowed, drawed, growed, knowed,* and *throwed* are preferred to *blew, drew, grew, knew,* and *threw,* forms which arouse at once the resentment of older mountain folk against offspring whose heads are turned by "new-fangled foolishness they larn 'em down thar at that thar schoolhouse."

15. But certain persistent perversities in the use of verbs are also widespread. Strong verbs are often weakened, irregular verbs made regular. The past and past participle of *born* become *borned; bust, busted; catch, catched* (pronounced *ketch* and *ketched*); *hear, heared; drink, drinkened; mistake, mistakened; see, seed; seek, seeked; shine, shined; take, takened; teach, teached; win, winned.*

16. The *-d* and *-ed* endings of past forms of verbs are frequently pronounced *-t*, particularly when the ending is preceded by *l, m, n,* or *r*. A few such verbs are *bound, bount; held, helt; burned, burnt; killed, kilt; dreamed, dremt; leaned, lent; found, fount; spun, spunt; feared, feart; scared, skeart; worried, worrit*. The mountaineer's preference for *t* over *d* in conjunction with nasal sounds sometimes results in *wutn't, cutn't,* and *shutn't*. *Wasn't* often becomes *wudn't*. The hyper-urban returned migrant whose head has been turned by outlanders' ways may use *idn't, hadn't* and *habn't* for *isn't, hasn't,* and *haven't*, partly perhaps out of deference to his natural preference for *ain't* and *hain't*.

17. Past participles used as direct adjectives are often given *-en* or *-ed* endings: *blood-shotten eyes, store-boughten shoes, a growned man, a forsakened house, a knowned fact.*

18. The ease with which mountain folk convert nouns and adjectives to verbs has long fascinated outsiders. The mountain farmer talks of raising enough corn to "bread" his family and enough "roughness" to "winter" his "brutes." He "pastures" his cows, "stables" his mules, and "pens" his hogs. He "grasses" a field after he has "corned" it for a few years, and he "sleds" his crops off the mountains. He cradles his oats and "sies" ("scythes") his clover, logs his poplars and "cross-ties" his whiteoaks, "poles" his fences and "ciders" his apples (when he doesn't "brandy" them). His sons go "musickin'" on Saturday night and go "galin'" on Sunday. His preacher may not be "scholared" enough to read the Bible, but the hill farmer is "pleasured" to "listen at 'im" if he is a "scriptored" preacher. If his neighbor Judd Sizemore "flouts" him, he "Judd Sizemores" Judd Sizemore.

19. Occasionally the outsider is surprised to hear some verb he has never heard before. The farmer's wife might complain that the "biddies" and goslings around the kitchen door "might' nigh" drive her

crazy with their "infernal and everlastin' whoodlin' " because she has "disremembered" to feed them. "A body'd thank they was beholdenst to the critters to listen to 'em cheep the endurin' day from the crack o' dawn to dusky dark. Betwixt the noisy critters and the whinkin' youngens a body don't git much peace." The farmer scolds the child for taking out more "grub" than he can eat and "a-smoulin' around over it and a-mommickin' it up till nobody else can stommick it." His daughters rise early on Sunday to "trig" themselves up in "Sunday-go-to-meetin' duds." They "take and do" strange things to their hair, inspect each other carefully to see that their "pettiskirts" don't "gyarp," and go "waltzin' " out to church. Woe to the daring swain who attempts to "buss" one unawares if he is not prepared to be "biffed one on the snoot."

20. One rarely finds a mountaineer today whose speech would include all of the verb usages discussed here. I knew a deputy sheriff in a Kentucky mountain community who came as close to full usage of these verb forms as anyone I have ever known. Unable to read and write, he was unselfconscious and free and easy while speaking. Once, in exchanging the time of day with him, I observed that I had not seen him at the last basketball game. He responded:

21. "The high shurf sent me down to Oliver Hill to git a feller down thar. The shurf got word that he 'uz a stayin' at his sister's off down thar sommers."

22. "Well, did you get him?"

23. "Yeah. I got off'n the train thar at the deep-po and walked over to the hoe-tell jest across the yard. I jest happened to look up the street and I seed 'im a-comin'. As soon as I seed 'im, I knowed I had 'im. So I jest stepped behind a little house-of-a-thang and clomb upon a bar'l a-settin' thar. When he got up fernenst me, I rech out and cotch holdst of 'im and says, 'You come and go along wi' me.' "

24. "Did you have any trouble with him?"

25. "Nary bit. He begin to pull back, and I says, 'You want me to sqush yer head wi' this hyar .45?' He jest muled right down. I popped the handcuffs on 'im and brung 'im back on the next train. He's down hyar in jail now."

A. Heard bouchu did somp'n wrong. Wachu did?
B. Nothin.
A. Whas nothin?

B. I dunno.
A. Becha *do* know. Dya know?
B. No.
A. Now?
B. No.
A. (Pause) Bill, where ya went today?
B. Noplace.
A. Hikin?
B. No.
A. Where's you'n Steve?
B. Nowhere.
A. Yall ain going nowhere taday?
B. No.
A. Where yall goin?
B. Nowhere.
A. Steve said yalluz goin someplace.
B. Thass nah right.
A. Steve tell a lie?
B. Yeah.
A. Wann Steve fruh tutor?
B. No.
A. Y'goin, Bill, frah yer tutor?
B. Yeah . . . no.
A. Wann Maggi?
B. No . . . yeah.
A. Ya wann Maggie.
B. Yeah.
A. Ya wann Steve?
B. No.
A. Who ya want?
B. N'body.
A. Ya need somp-body.
B. Nah I don.
A. Ya need Maggie?
B. Yeah.
A. Wann Larry?
B. Yeah.
A. Wann Roger?
B. Yeah.
A. Ya wann . . . ya wann . . . ya wann . . . Patrick?
B. Yeah.
A. Wann Gary?
B. Yeah.
A. Who else d'yah wann? Name me everbody ya know.
B. Nobody else.

A. Cher mothuh?
B. Yeah.
A. Cher fathuh?
B. Yeah.
A. Cher sissuhs?
B. Yeah.
A. Wann Stanley?
B. Yeah.
A. Wann—
B. No!
A. No, ya wann—
B. No. No. Oh-oh-oh-oh-oh-oh. Ooooh!
    Oh-oh-oh-oh. . . . Ooooh!
    Oh, wooh-ooh, I wannchu, ooh, eh, ooh, eh.
A. Hurry up now, ooh heh!
    Hurry up, hurry up
    Com'n hurr-yup
    Hurr-yup, hurr-yup, hurry up yeah.
B. Gimme me, yeah, yeah,
    Gimme one yeah-heh-haah. *(Reaches for the other's cigarettes)*
A. Hurr-yup.
B. Com'n cool joick,
    Com'n-ah cool joick,
    Want one, gimme a light,
    Gimme a light, c'mon.
A. Woick it on, baby, woick it on out.
B. Gimme a light, Ah-thuh,
    Gimme a li—hey! you cain smoke eithuh! *(Grabs Arthur's cigarette)*
A. You cain git'm! Louie, com'n ov-a-here, mon. Gimme suh! Grimmer s'matches, eh, eh, eh—
B. Coil joick,
    Coil joick,
    Canned heat. Wann summer cigret?
A. Hell, no, ain't none-a-theh!
B. Ever-thin in this place is mine and-a-runnit!
    Now-ee run datoo, kit,
    Gicher hans off't cheer fuh uh buhn yuh, yeah,
    Yeah, yeah, she's a muv-eh, yeah, yeah, yeah,
A. Ain goanta school no more,
    Cuz its a honky-jonk,
    Nothin but a jonk, yeah.

           Conversation between two second-graders
           from the same ghetto school. One is white,
           the other black.

In recent years a few scholars, Marshall McLuhan and Edmund Carpenter among them, have suggested not only that the book as we know it is out-of-date, but that it was a severely limited form to begin with. In the following article Carpenter says why. Whether or not one quite agrees (ironically, McLuhan and Carpenter have been influential primarily on account of their books), Carpenter's final question, paragraph 61, is one which students of language and literature will want to consider.

The New Languages

Edmund Carpenter

Brain of the New World,
What a task is thine,
To formulate the modern
. . . to recast poems, churches, art

WHITMAN

English is a mass medium. All languages are mass media. The new mass media—film, radio, TV—are new languages, their grammars as yet unknown. Each codifies reality differently; each conceals a unique metaphysics. Linguists tell us it's possible to say anything in any language if you use enough words or images, but there's rarely time; the natural course is for a culture to exploit its media biases.

2. Writing, for example, didn't record oral language; it was a new language, which the spoken word came to imitate. Writing encouraged an analytical mode of thinking with emphasis upon lineality. Oral languages tended to be polysynthetic, composed of great, tight conglomerates, like twisted knots, within which images were juxtaposed, inseparably fused; written communications consisted of little words chronologically ordered. Subject became distinct from verb, adjective from noun, thus separating actor from action, essence from form. Where preliterate man imposed form diffidently, temporarily—for such transitory forms lived but temporarily on the tip of his tongue, in the living situation—the printed word was inflexible, permanent, in touch with eternity: it embalmed truth for posterity.

3. This embalming process froze language, eliminated the art of ambiguity, made puns "the lowest form of wit," destroyed word linkages. The word became a static symbol, applicable to and separate from that which it symbolized. It now belonged to the objective world; it could be seen. Now came the distinction between being and meaning, the dispute as to whether the Eucharist *was* or only *signified* the body of the Sacrifice. The word became a neutral symbol, no longer an inextricable part of a creative process.

4. Gutenberg completed the process. The manuscript page with pictures, colors, correlation between symbol and space, gave way to uniform type, the black-and-white page, read silently, alone. The format of the book favored lineal expression, for the argument ran like a thread from cover to cover: subject to verb to object, sentence to sentence, paragraph to paragraph, chapter to chapter, carefully structured from beginning to end, with value embedded in the climax. This was not true of great poetry and drama, which retained multiperspective, but it was true of most books, particularly texts, histories, autobiographies, novels. Events were arranged chronologically and hence, it was assumed, causally; relationship, not being, was valued. The author became an *authority;* his data were serious, that is, *serially* organized. Such data, if sequentially ordered and printed, conveyed value and truth; arranged any other way, they were suspect.

5. The newspaper format brought an end to book culture. It offers short, discrete articles that give important facts first and then taper off to incidental details, which may be, and often are, eliminated by the make-up man. The fact that reporters cannot control the length of their articles means that, in writing them, emphasis can't be placed on structure, at least in the traditional linear sense, with climax or conclusion at the end. Everything has to be captured in the headline; from there it goes down the pyramid to incidentals. In fact there is often more in the headline than in the article; occasionally, no article at all accompanies the banner headline.

6. The position and size of articles on the front page are determined by interest and importance, not content. Unrelated reports from Moscow, Sarawak, London, and Ittipik are juxtaposed; time and space, as separate concepts, are destroyed and the *here* and *now* presented as a single Gestalt. Subway readers consume everything on the front page, then turn to page 2 to read, in incidental order, continuations. A Toronto banner headline ran: TOWNSEND TO MARRY PRINCESS; directly beneath this was a second headline: *Fabian Says This May Not Be Sex Crime.* This went unnoticed by eyes and minds conditioned to consider each newspaper item in isolation.

7. Such a format lends itself to simultaneity, not chronology or lineality. Items abstracted from a total situation aren't arranged in casual sequence, but presented holistically, as raw experience. The front page is a cosmic *Finnegans Wake.*

8. The disorder of the newspaper throws the reader into a producer role. The reader has to process the news himself; he has to co-create, to cooperate in the creation of the work. The newspaper format calls for the direct participation of the consumer.

9. In magazines, where a writer more frequently controls the length of his article, he can, if he wishes, organize it in traditional style, but the majority don't. An increasingly popular presentation is the printed symposium, which is little more than collected opinions, pro and con. The magazine format as a whole opposes lineality; its pictures lack tenses. In *Life*, extremes are juxtaposed: space ships and prehistoric monsters, Flemish monasteries and dope addicts. It creates a sense of urgency and uncertainty: the next page is unpredictable. One encounters rapidly a riot in Teheran, a Hollywood marriage, the wonders of the Eisenhower administration, a two-headed calf, a party on Jones beach, all sandwiched between ads. The eye takes in the page as a whole (readers may pretend this isn't so, but the success of advertising suggests it is), and the page—indeed, the whole magazine— becomes a single Gestalt where association, though not causal, is often lifelike.

10. The same is true of the other new languages. Both radio and TV offer short, unrelated programs, interrupted between and within by commercials. I say "interrupted," being myself an anachronism of book culture, but my children don't regard them as interruptions, as breaking continuity. Rather, they regard them as part of a whole, and their reaction is neither one of annoyance nor one of indifference. The ideal news broadcast has half a dozen speakers from as many parts of the world on as many subjects. The London correspondent doesn't comment on what the Washington correspondent has just said; he hasn't even heard him.

11. The child is right in not regarding commercials as interruptions. For the only time anyone smiles on TV is in commercials. The rest of life, in news broadcasts and soap operas, is presented as so horrible that the only way to get through life is to buy this product: then you'll smile. Aesop never wrote a clearer fable. It's heaven and hell brought up to date: Hell in the headline, Heaven in the ad. Without the other, neither has meaning.

12. There's pattern in these new media—not line, but knot; not lineality or causality or chronology, nothing that leads to a desired climax; but a Gordian knot without antecedents or results, containing within itself carefully selected elements, juxtaposed, inseparably fused; a knot that can't be untied to give the long, thin cord of lineality.

13. This is especially true of ads that never present an ordered, sequential, rational argument but simply present the product associated with desirable things or attitudes. Thus Coca-Cola is shown held by a beautiful blonde, who sits in a Cadillac, surrounded by bronze, muscular admirers, with the sun shining overhead. By repetition these elements become associated, in our minds, into a pattern of sufficient cohesion so that one element can magically evoke the others. If we think of ads as designed solely to sell products, we miss their main effect: to increase pleasure in the consumption of the product. Coca-Cola is far more than a cooling drink; the consumer participates, vicariously, in a much larger experience. In Africa, in Melanesia, to drink a Coke is to participate in the American way of life.

14. Of the new languages, TV comes closest to drama and ritual. It combines music and art, language and gesture, rhetoric and color. It favors simultaneity of visual and auditory images. Cameras focus not on speakers but on persons spoken to or about; the audience *hears* the accuser but *watches* the accused. In a single impression it hears the prosecutor, watches the trembling hands of the big-town crook, and sees the look of moral indignation on Senator Tobey's face. This is real drama, in process, with the outcome uncertain. Print can't do this; it has a different bias.

15. Books and movies only pretend uncertainty, but live TV retains this vital aspect of life. Seen on TV, the fire in the 1952 Democratic Convention threatened briefly to become a conflagration; seen on newsreel, it was history, without potentiality.

16. The absence of uncertainty is no handicap to other media, if they are properly used, for their biases are different. Thus it's clear from the beginning that Hamlet is a doomed man, but, far from detracting in interest, this heightens the sense of tragedy.

17. Now, one of the results of the time-space duality that developed in Western culture, principally from the Renaissance on, was a separation within the arts. Music, which created symbols in time, and graphic art, which created symbols in space, became separate pursuits, and men gifted in one rarely pursued the other. Dance and ritual, which inherently combined them, fell in popularity. Only in drama did they remain united.

18. It is significant that of the four new media, the three most recent are dramatic media, particularly TV, which combines language, music, art, dance. They don't, however, exercise the same freedom with time that the stage dares practice. An intricate plot, employing flash backs, multiple time perspectives and overlays, intelligible on the stage, would mystify on the screen. The audience has no time to think back, to establish relations between early hints and subsequent discoveries. The picture passes before the eyes too quickly; there are no intervals in which to take stock of what has happened and make conjectures of what is going to happen. The observer is in a more passive state, less interested in subtleties. Both TV and film are nearer to narrative and depend much more upon the episodic. An intricate time construction can be done in film, but in fact rarely is. The soliloquies of *Richard III* belong on the stage; the film audience was unprepared for them. On stage Ophelia's death was described by three separate groups: one hears the announcement and watches the reactions simultaneously. On film the camera flatly shows her drowned where "a willow lies aslant a brook."

19. Media differences such as these mean that it's not simply a question of communicating a single idea in different ways but that a given idea or insight belongs primarily, though not exclusively, to one medium, and can be gained or communicated best through that medium.

20. Thus the book was ideally suited for discussing evolution and progress. Both belonged, almost exclusively, to book culture. Like a book, the idea of progress was an abstracting, organizing principle for the interpretation and comprehension of the incredibly complicated record of human experience. The sequence of events was believed to have a direction, to follow a given course along an axis of time; it was held that civilization, like the reader's eye (in J. B. Bury's words), "has moved, is moving, and will move in a desirable direction. Knowledge will advance, and with that advance, reason and decency must increasingly prevail among men." Here we see the three main elements of book lineality: the line, the point moving along that line, and its movement toward a desirable goal.

21. The Western conception of a definite moment in the present, of the present as a definite moment or a definite point, so important in book-dominated languages, is absent, to my knowledge, in oral languages. Absent as well, in oral societies, are such animating and controlling ideas as Western individualism and three-dimensional perspective, both related to this conception of the definite moment, and both nourished, probably bred, by book culture.

22. Each medium selects its ideas. TV is a tiny box into which people are crowded and must live; film gives us the wide world. With its huge screen, film is perfectly suited for social drama, Civil War panoramas, the sea, land erosion, Cecil B. DeMille spectaculars. In contrast, the TV screen has room for two, at the most three, faces comfortably. TV is closer to stage, yet different. Paddy Chayefsky writes:

> The theatre audience is far away from the actual action of the drama. They cannot see the silent reactions of the players. They must be told in a loud voice what is going on. The plot movement from one scene to another must be marked, rather than gently shaded as is required in television. In television, however, you can dig into the most humble, ordinary relationships; the relationship of bourgeois children to their mother, of middle-class husband to his wife, of white-collar father to his secretary—in short, the relationships of the people. We relate to each other in an incredibly complicated manner. There is far more exciting drama in the reasons why a man gets married than in why he murders someone. The man who is unhappy in his job, the wife who thinks of a lover, the girl who wants to get into television, your father, your mother, sister, brothers, cousins, friends—all these are better subjects for drama than Iago. What makes a man ambitious? Why does a girl always try to steal her kid sister's boy friends? Why

does your uncle attend his annual class reunion faithfully every year?
Why do you always find it depressing to visit your father? These are
the substances of good television drama; and the deeper you probe
into and examine the twisted, semi-formed complexes of emotional
entanglements, the more exciting your writing becomes.

23. This is the primary reason, I believe, why Greek drama is more
readily adapted to TV than to film. The boxed-in quality of live TV
lends itself to static literary tragedy with greater ease than does
the elastic, energetic, expandable movie. Guthrie's recent movie of
Oedipus favored the panoramic shot rather than the selective eye. It
consisted of a succession of tableaux, a series of elaborate, unnatural
poses. The effect was of congested groups of people moving in tight
formation as though they had trained for it by living for days together
in a self-service elevator. With the lines, "I grieve for the City, and for
myself and you . . . and walk through endless ways of thought," the
inexorable tragedy moved to its horrible "come to realize" climax as
though everyone were stepping on everyone else's feet.

24. The tight, necessary conventions of live TV were more sympa-
thetic to Sophocles in the Aluminum Hour's *Antigone*. Restrictions of
space are imposed on TV as on the Greek stage by the size and inflexi-
bility of the studio. Squeezed by physical limitations, the producer
was forced to expand the viewer's imagination with ingenious devices.

25. When T. S. Eliot adapted *Murder in the Cathedral* for film, he
noted a difference in realism between cinema and stage:

> Cinema, even where fantasy is introduced, is much more realistic
> than the stage. Especially in an historical picture, the setting, the
> costume, and the way of life represented have to be accurate. Even a
> minor anachronism is intolerable. On the stage much more can be
> overlooked or forgiven; and indeed, an excessive care for accuracy of
> historical detail can become burdensome and distracting. In watching
> a stage performance, the member of the audience is in direct contact
> with the actor playing a part. In looking at a film, we are much more
> passive; as audience, we contribute less. We are seized with the illu-
> sion that we are observing an actual event, or at least a series of
> photographs of the actual event; and nothing must be allowed to break
> this illusion. Hence the precise attention to detail.

26. If two men are on a stage in a theatre, the dramatist is obliged to
motivate their presence; he has to account for their existing on the

stage at all. Whereas if a camera is following a figure down a street or is turned to any object whatever, there is no need for a reason to be provided. Its grammar contains that power of statement of motivation, no matter what it looks at.

In the theatre, the spectator sees the enacted scene as a whole in space, always seeing the whole of the space. The stage may present only one corner of a large hall, but that corner is always totally visible all through the scene. And the spectator always sees that scene from a fixed, unchanging distance and from an angle of vision that doesn't change. Perspective may change from scene to scene, but within one scene it remains constant. Distance never varies.

27. But in film and TV, distance and angle constantly shift. The same scene is shown in multiple perspective and focus. The viewer sees it from here, there, then over here; finally he is drawn inexorably into it, becomes part of it. He ceases to be a spectator. Balázs writes:

> Although we sit in our seats, we do not see Romeo and Juliet from there. We look up into Juliet's balcony with Romeo's eyes and look down on Romeo with Juliet's. Our eye and with it our consciousness is identified with the characters in the film, we look at the world out of their eyes and have no angle of vision of our own. We walk amid crowds, ride, fly or fall with the hero and if one character looks into the other's eyes, he looks into our eyes from the screen, for, our eyes are in the camera and become identical with the gaze of the characters. They see with our eyes. Herein lies the psychological act of identification. Nothing like this "identification" has ever occurred as the effect of any other system of art and it is here that the film manifests its absolute artistic novelty.
>
> . . . Not only can we see, in the isolated "shots" of a scene, the very atoms of life and their innermost secrets revealed at close quarters, but we can do so without any of the intimate secrecy being lost, as always happens in the exposure of a stage performance or of a painting. The new theme which the new means of expression of film art revealed was not a hurricane at sea or the eruption of a volcano: it was perhaps a solitary tear slowly welling up in the corner of a human eye.
>
> . . . Not to speak does not mean that one has nothing to say. Those who do not speak may be brimming over with emotions which can be expressed only in forms and pictures, in gesture and play of feature. The man of visual culture uses these not as substitutes for words, as a deaf-mute uses his fingers.

28. The gestures of visual man are not intended to convey concepts that can be expressed in words, but inner experiences, non-rational emotions, which would still remain unexpressed when everything that can be told has been told. Such emotions lie in the deepest levels. They cannot be approached by words that are mere reflections of concepts, any more than musical experiences can be expressed in rational concepts. Facial expression is a human experience rendered immediately visible without the intermediary of word. It is Turgenev's "living truth of the human face."

29. Printing rendered illegible the faces of men. So much could be read from paper that the method of conveying meaning by facial expression fell into desuetude. The press grew to be the main bridge over which the more remote interhuman spiritual exchanges took place; the immediate, the personal, the inner, died. There was no longer need for the subtler means of expression provided by the body. The face became immobile; the inner life, still. Wells that dry up are wells from which no water is dipped.

30. Just as radio helped bring back inflection in speech, so film and TV are aiding us in the recovery of gesture and facial awareness—a rich, colorful language, conveying moods and emotions, happenings and characters, even thoughts, none of which could be properly packaged in words. If film had remained silent for another decade, how much faster this change might have been!

31. Feeding the product of one medium through another medium creates a new product. When Hollywood buys a novel, it buys a title and the publicity associated with it: nothing more. Nor should it.

32. Each of the four versions of the *Caine Mutiny*—book, play, movie, TV—had a different hero: Willie Keith, the lawyer Greenwald, the United States Navy, and Captain Queeg, respectively. Media and audience biases were clear. Thus the book told, in lengthy detail, of the growth and making of Ensign William Keith, American man, while the movie camera with its colorful shots of ships and sea, unconsciously favored the Navy as hero, a bias supported by the fact the Navy cooperated with the movie makers. Because of stage limitations, the play was confined, except for the last scene, to the courtroom, and favored the defense counsel as hero. The TV show, aimed at a mass audience, emphasized patriotism, authority, allegiance. More important, the cast was reduced to the principals and the plot to its principles; the real moral problem—the refusal of subordinates to assist an incompetent, unpopular superior—was clear, whereas in the book it was lost under detail, in the film under scenery. Finally, the New York play, with its audience slanted toward Expense Account patronage—Mr. Sampson, Western Sales Manager for the Cavity Drill Company—became a morality play with Willie Keith, innocent American youth, torn between two influences: Keefer, clever author but moral cripple, and Greenwald, equally brilliant but reliable, a businessman's intellectual. Greenwald saves Willie's soul.

33. The film *Moby Dick* was in many ways an improvement on the book, primarily because of its explicitness. For *Moby Dick* is one of those admittedly great classics, like *Robinson Crusoe* or Kafka's *Trial*, whose plot and situation, as distilled apart from the book by time and familiarity, are actually much more imposing than the written book itself. It's the drama of Ahab's defiance rather than Melville's uncharted leviathan meanderings that is the greatness of *Moby Dick*. On film, instead of laborious tacks through leagues of discursive interruptions, the most vivid descriptions of whales and whaling become part of the action. On film, the viewer was constantly aboard ship: each scene an instantaneous shot of whaling life, an effect achieved in the book only by illusion, by constant, detailed reference. From start to finish, all the action of the film served to develop what was most central to the theme—a man's magnificent and blasphemous pride in attempting to destroy the brutal, unreasoning force that maims him and turns man-made order into chaos. Unlike the book, the film gave a spare, hard, compelling dramatization, free of self-conscious symbolism.

34. Current confusion over the respective roles of the new media comes largely from a misconception of their function. They are artforms, not substitutes for human contact. Insofar as they attempt to usurp speech and personal, living relations, they harm. This, of course, has long been one of the problems of book culture, at least during the time of its monopoly of Western middle-class thought. But this was never a legitimate function of books, nor of any other medium. Whenever a medium goes claim jumping, trying to work areas where it is ill-suited, conflicts occur with other media, or, more accurately, between the vested interests controlling each. But, when media simply exploit their own formats, they become complementary and cross-fertile.

35. Some people who have no one around talk to cats, and you can hear their voices in the next room, and they sound silly, because the

cat won't answer, but that suffices to maintain the illusion that their world is made up of living people, while it is not. Mechanized mass media reverse this: now mechanical cats talk to humans. There's no genuine feedback.

36. This charge is often leveled by academicians at the new media, but it holds equally for print. The open-mouthed, glaze-eyed TV spectator is merely the successor of the passive, silent, lonely reader whose head moved back and forth like a shuttlecock.

38. When we read, another person thinks for us: we merely repeat his mental process. The greater part of the work of thought is done for us. This is why it relieves us to take up a book after being occupied by our own thoughts. In reading, the mind is only the playground for another's ideas. People who spend most of their lives in reading often lose the capacity for thinking, just as those who always ride forget how to walk. Some people read themselves stupid. Chaplin did a wonderful take-off of this in *City Lights*, when he stood up on a chair to eat the endless confetti that he mistook for spaghetti.

39. Eliot remarks: "It is often those writers whom we are lucky enough to know whose books we can ignore; and the better we know them personally, the less need we may feel to read what they write."

40. Frank O'Connor highlights a basic distinction between oral and written traditions: " 'By the hokies, there was a man in this place one time by name of Ned Sullivan, and he had a queer thing happen to him late one night and he coming up the Valley Road from Durlas.' This is how a folk story begins, or should begin. . . . Yet that is how no printed short story should begin, because such a story seems tame when you remove it from its warm nest by the cottage fire, from the sense of an audience with its interjections, and the feeling of terror at what may lurk in the darkness outside."

41. Face-to-face discourse is not as selective, abstract, nor explicit as any mechanical medium; it probably comes closer to communicating an unabridged situation than any of them, and, insofar as it exploits the give-take of dynamic relationship, it's clearly the most indispensably human one.

42. Of course, there can be personal involvement in the other media. When Richardson's *Pamela* was serialized in 1741, it aroused such interest that in one English town, upon receipt of the last installment, the church bell announced that virtue had been rewarded. Radio stations have reported receiving quantities of baby clothes and bassinets when, in a soap opera, a heroine had a baby. One of the commonest phrases used by devoted listeners to daytime serials is that they "visited with" Aunt Jenny or Big Sister. BBC and *News Chronicle* report cases of women viewers who kneel before TV sets to kiss male announcers good night.

43. Each medium, if its bias is properly exploited, reveals and communicates a unique aspect of reality, of truth. Each offers a different perspective, a way of seeing an otherwise hidden dimension of reality. It's not a question of one reality being true, the others distortions. One allows us to see from here, another from there, a third from still another perspective; taken together they give us a more complete whole, a greater truth. New essentials are brought to the fore, including those made invisible by the "blinders" of old languages.

44. This is why the preservation of book culture is as important as the development of TV. This is why new languages, instead of destroying old ones, serve as a stimulant to them. Only monopoly is destroyed. When actor-collector Edward G. Robinson was battling actor-collector Vincent Price on art on TV's *$64,000 Challenge*, he was asked how the quiz had affected his life; he answered petulantly, "Instead of looking at the pictures in my art books, I now have to read them." Print, along with all old languages, including speech, has profited enormously from the development of the new media. "The more the arts develop," writes E. M. Forster, "the more they depend on each other for definition. We will borrow from painting first and call it pattern. Later we will borrow from music and call it rhythm."

46. The appearance of a new medium often frees older media for creative effort. They no longer have to serve the interests of power and profit. Elia Kazan, discussing the American theatre, says:

> Take 1900–1920. The theatre flourished all over the country. It had no competition. The box office boomed. The top original fare it had to offer was *The Girl of the Golden West*. Its bow to culture was fusty productions of Shakespeare. . . . Came the moving pictures. The theatre had to be better or go under. It got better. It got so spectacularly better so fast that in 1920–1930 you wouldn't have recognized it. Perhaps it was an accident that Eugene O'Neill appeared at that moment—but it was no accident that in that moment of strange competition, the theatre had room for him. Because it was disrupted and hard pressed, it made room for his experiments, his unheard-of subjects, his passion, his power. There was room for him to grow to his full stature. And there was freedom for the talents that came after his.

47. Yet a new language is rarely welcomed by the old. The oral tradition distrusted writing, manuscript culture was contemptuous of printing, book culture hated the press, that "slag-heap of hellish passions," as one 19th century scholar called it. A father, protesting to a Boston newspaper about crime and scandal, said he would rather see his children "in their graves while pure in innocence, than dwelling with pleasure upon these reports, which have grown so bold."

48. What really disturbed book-oriented people wasn't the sensationalism of the newspaper, but its nonlineal format, its nonlineal codifications of experience. The motto of conservative academicians became: *Hold that line!*

49. A new language lets us see with the fresh, sharp eyes of the child; it offers the pure joy of discovery. I was recently told a story about a Polish couple who, though long resident in Toronto, retained many of the customs of their homeland. Their son despaired of ever getting his father to buy a suit cut in style or getting his mother to take an interest in Canadian life. Then he bought them a TV set, and in a matter of months a major change took place. One evening the mother remarked that "Edith Piaf is the latest thing on Broadway," and the father appeared in "the kind of suit executives wear on TV." For years the father had passed this same suit in store windows and seen it both in advertisements and on living men, but not until he saw it on TV did it become meaningful. This same statement goes for all media: each offers a unique presentation of reality, which when new has a freshness and clarity that is extraordinarily powerful.

50. This is especially true of TV. We say, "We have a radio" but "We have television"—as if something had happened to us. It's no longer "The skin you love to touch" but "The Nylon that loves to touch you." We don't watch TV; it watches us: it guides us. Magazines and newspapers no longer convey "information" but offer ways of seeing things. They have abandoned realism as too easy: they substitute themselves for realism. *Life* is totally advertisements: its articles package and sell emotions and ideas just as its paid ads sell commodities.

51. Several years ago, a group of us at the University of Toronto undertook the following experiment: 136 students were divided, on the basis of their over-all academic standing of the previous year, into four equal groups who either (1) heard and saw a lecture delivered in a TV studio, (2) heard and saw this same lecture on a TV screen, (3) heard it over the radio, or (4) read it in manuscript. Thus there were, in the CBC studios, four controlled groups who simultaneously received a single lecture and then immediately wrote an identical examination to test both understanding and retention of content. Later the experiment was repeated, using three similar groups; this time the same lecture was (1) delivered in a classroom, (2) presented as a film (using the kinescope) in a small theatre, and (3) again read in print. The actual mechanics of the experiment were relatively simple, but the problem of writing the script for the lecture led to a consideration of the resources and limitations of the dramatic forms involved.

52. It immediately became apparent that no matter how the script was written and the show produced, it would be slanted in various ways for and against each of the media involved; no show could be produced that did not contain these biases, and the only real common denominator was the simultaneity of presentation. For each communication channel codifies reality differently and thus influences, to a surprising degree, the content of the message communicated. A medium is not simply an envelope that carries any letter; it is itself a major part of that message. We therefore decided not to exploit the full resources of any one medium, but to try to chart a middle-of-the-road course between all of them.

53. The lecture that was finally produced dealt with linguistic codifications of reality and metaphysical concepts underlying grammatical systems. It was chosen because it concerned a field in which few students could be expected to have prior knowledge; moreover, it offered opportunities for the use of gesture. The cameras moved throughout the lecture, and took close-ups where relevant. No other visual aids were used, nor were shots taken of the audience while the lecture was in progress. Instead, the cameras simply focused on the speaker for 27 minutes.

54. The first difference we found between a classroom and a TV lecture was the brevity of the latter. The classroom lecture, if not ideally, at least in practice, sets a slower pace. It's verbose, repetitive. It allows for greater elaboration and permits the lecturer to take up several *related* points. TV, however, is stripped right down; there's less time for qualifications or alternative interpretations and only time enough for *one* point. (Into 27 minutes we put the meat of a two-hour classroom lecture.) The ideal TV speaker states his point and then brings out different facets of it by a variety of illustrations. But the classroom lecturer is less subtle and, to the agony of the better students, repeats and repeats his identical points in the hope, perhaps, that ultimately no student will miss them, or perhaps simply because he is dull. Teachers have had captive audiences for so long that few are equipped to compete for attention via the new media.

55. The next major difference noted was the abstracting role of each medium, beginning with print. Edmund M. Morgan, Harvard Law Professor, writes:

> One who forms his opinion from the reading of any record alone is prone to err, because the printed page fails to produce the impression or convey the idea which the spoken word produced or conveyed. The writer has read charges to the jury which he had previously heard delivered, and has been amazed to see an oral deliverance which indicated a strong bias appear on the printed page as an ideally impartial exposition. He has seen an appellate court solemnly declare the testimony of a witness to be especially clear and convincing which the trial judge had orally characterized as the most abject perjury.

56. Selectivity of print and radio are perhaps obvious enough, but we are less conscious of it in TV, partly because we have already been conditioned to it by the shorthand of film. Balázs writes:

> A man hurries to a railway station to take leave of his beloved. We see him on the platform. We cannot see the train, but the questing eyes of the man show us that his beloved is already seated in the train. We see only a close-up of the man's face, we see it twitch as if startled and then strips of light and shadow, light and shadow flit across it in quickening rhythm. Then tears gather in the eyes and that ends the scene. We are expected to know what happened and today we do know, but when I first saw this film in Berlin, I did not at once understand the end of this scene. Soon, however, everyone knew what had happened: the train had started and it was the lamps in its compartment which had thrown their light on the man's face as they glided past ever faster and faster.

57. As in a movie theatre, only the screen is illuminated, and, on it, only points of immediate relevance are portrayed; everything else is eliminated. This explicitness makes TV not only personal but forceful. That's why stage hands in a TV studio watch the show over floor monitors, rather than watch the actual performance before their eyes.

58. The script of the lecture, timed for radio, proved too long for TV. Visual aids and gestures on TV not only allow the elimination of certain words, but require a unique script. The ideal radio delivery stresses pitch and intonation to make up for the absence of the visual. That flat, broken speech in "sidewalk interviews" is the speech of a person untrained in radio delivery.

59. The results of the examination showed that TV had won, followed by lecture, film, radio, and finally print. Eight months later the test was readministered to the bulk of the students who had taken it the first time. Again it was found that there were significant differences between the groups exposed to different media, and these differences were the same as those on the first test, save for the studio group, an uncertain group because of the chaos of the lecture conditions, which had moved from last to second place. Finally, two years later, the experiment was repeated, with major modifications, using students at Ryerson Institute. Marshall McLuhan reports:

> In this repeat performance, pains were taken to allow each medium full play of its possibilities with reference to the subject, just as in the earlier experiment each medium was neutralized as much as possible. Only the mimeograph form remained the same in each experiment. Here we added a printed form in which an imaginative typographical layout was followed. The lecturer used the blackboard and permitted discussion. Radio and TV employed dramatization, sound effects and graphics. In the examination, radio easily topped TV. Yet, as in the first experiment, both radio and TV manifested a decisive advantage over the lecture and written forms. As a conveyor both of ideas and information, TV was, in this second experiment, apparently enfeebled by the deployment of its dramatic resources, whereas radio benefited from such lavishness. "Technology is explicitness," writes Lyman Bryson. Are both radio and TV more explicit than writing or lecture? Would a greater explicitness, if inherent in these media, account for the ease with which they top other modes of performance?

60. Announcement of the results of the first experiment evoked considerable interest. Advertising agencies circulated the results with the comment that here, at last, was scientific proof of the superiority of TV. This was unfortunate and missed the main point, for the results didn't indicate the superiority of one medium over others. They merely directed attention toward differences between them, differences so great as to be of kind rather than degree. Some CBC officials were furious, not because TV won, but because print lost.

61. The problem has been falsely seen as democracy *vs.* the mass media. But the mass media *are* democracy. The book itself was the first mechanical mass medium. What is really being asked, of course, is: can books' monopoly of knowledge survive the challenge of the new languages? The answer is: no. What should be asked is: what can print do better than any other medium and is that worth doing?

Our new electric technology that extends our senses and nerves in a global embrace has large implications for the future of language. Electric technology does not need words any more than the digital computer needs numbers. Electricity points the way to an extension of the process of consciousness itself, on a world scale, and without any verbalization whatever. Such a state of collective awareness may have been the preverbal condition of men. Language as the technology of human extension, whose powers of division and separation we know so well, may have been the "Tower of Babel" by which men sought to scale the highest heavens. Today computers hold out the promise of a means of instant translation of any code or language into any other code or language. The computer, in short, promises by technology a Pentecostal condition of universal understanding and unity. The next logical step would seem to be, not to translate, but to by-pass languages in favor of a general cosmic consciousness which might be very like the collective unconscious dreamt of by Bergson. The condition of "weightlessness" that biologists say promises a physical immortality, may be paralleled by the condition of speechlessness that could confer a perpetuity of collective harmony and peace.

Marshall McLuhan,

Understanding Media

"Conscious mind; canicular tales; egregious an argument (whenas egregious is never used in English but in the extreme ill part); ingenuity; jovial mind; valorous authors; inkhorn adventures; inkhorn pads; putative opinions; putative artists; energetical persuasions; rascality; materiality; artificiality; fantasticality; divine entelechy; loud mentery; deceitful perfidy; addicted to theory; the world's great incendiary; sirenized furies; sovereignty immense; abundant cautels; cautelous and adventurous; cordial liquor; Catilinaries and Phillipics; perfunctory discourses; David's sweetness Olympic; the Idee high and deep abyss of excellence; the only unicorn of the Muses; the Aretinish mountain of huge exaggeration; the gracious law of amnesty; amicable terms; amicable end; effectuate; addoulce his melody; Magi; polymechany; extensively employed; precious trainment; novelettes; notoriety; negotiations; mechanician."

Nor are these all, for every third line hath some of this over-racked absonism. Nor do I altogether scum off all these as the new engendered foam of the English, but allow some of them for a need to fill up a verse—as "trainment," and one or two words more which the liberty of prose might well have spared. In a verse, when a word of three syllables cannot thrust in but sidelings, to joint him even we are oftentimes fain to borrow some less quarry of elocution from the Latin, always retaining this for a principle: that a leak of indesinence, as a leak in a ship, must needly be stopped with what matter soever.

Thomas Nashe,

listing and denouncing the new words and phrases introduced by a contemporary writer, from *Strange News of the Intercepting Certain Letters,* 1592.

George Orwell discusses the "collapse of language" in "Politics and the English Language." He does not mean "the collapse of grammar," nor the use of neologisms, nor the writing of colloquialisms. Instead, he accuses contemporary writers of two major sins: a staleness of imagery and a lack of precision, of saying more and meaning less. As he warns, "ready-made phrases . . . will construct your sentences for you . . . and at need they will perform the important service of partially concealing your meaning even from yourself." He claims that concealment is necessary because politically expedient, for if we think of "men dying" instead of "necessary executions" we may be roused to action—action which all governments deplore. Therefore, he says, "the whole tendency of modern prose is away from concreteness." However, he adds, the process of corruption is reversible. By following Orwell's instructions, searching for clarity, the language may be saved. Is "goobledygook" reversible? Can "governmentalese" still be translated into meaningful English?

Politics and the English Language

George Orwell

Most people who bother with the matter at all would admit that the English language is in a bad way, but it is generally assumed that we cannot by conscious action do anything about it. Our civilization is decadent and our language—so the argument runs—must inevitably share in the general collapse. It follows that any struggle against the abuse of language is a sentimental archaism, like preferring candles to electric light or hansom cabs to aeroplanes. Underneath this lies the half-conscious belief that language is a natural growth and not an instrument which we shape for our own purposes.

2. Now, it is clear that the decline of a language must ultimately have political and economic causes: it is not due simply to the bad influence of this or that individual writer. But an effect can become a cause, reinforcing the original cause and producing the same effect in an intensified form, and so on indefinitely. A man may take to drink because he feels himself to be a failure, and then fail all the more completely because he drinks. It is rather the same thing that is happening to the English language. It becomes ugly and inaccurate because our thoughts are foolish, but the slovenliness of our language makes it easier for us to have foolish thoughts. The point is that the process is reversible. Modern English, especially written English, is full of bad habits which spread by imitation and which can be avoided if one is willing to take the necessary trouble. If one gets rid of these habits one can think more clearly, and to think clearly is a necessary first step towards political regeneration: so that the fight against bad English is not frivolous and is not the exclusive concern of professional writers. I will come back to this presently, and I hope that by that time the meaning of what I have said here will have become clearer. Meanwhile, here are five specimens of the English language as it is now habitually written.

3. These five passages have not been picked out because they are especially bad—I could have quoted far worse if I had chosen— but because they illustrate various of the mental vices from which we now suffer. They are a little below the average, but are fairly representative samples. I number them so that I can refer back to them when necessary:

> (1) I am not, indeed, sure whether it is not true to say that the Milton who once seemed not unlike a seventeenth-century Shelley had not become, out of an experience ever more bitter in each year, more alien [*sic*] to the founder of that Jesuit sect which nothing could induce him to tolerate.
>
> Professor Harold Laski
(Essay in *Freedom of Expression*).

> (2) Above all, we cannot play ducks and drakes with a native battery of idioms which prescribes such egregious collocations of vocables as the Basic *put up with* for *tolerate* or *put at a loss* for *bewilder*.
>
> Professor Lancelot Hogben (*Interglossa*).

something else, or he is almost indifferent as to whether his words
mean anything or not. This mixture of vagueness and sheer incompe-
tence is the most marked characteristic of modern English prose, and
especially of any kind of political writing. As soon as certain topics
are raised, the concrete melts into the abstract and no one seems able
to think of turns of speech that are not hackneyed: prose consists less
and less of *words* chosen for the sake of their meaning, and more and
more of *phrases* tacked together like the sections of a prefabricated
hen-house. I list below, with notes and examples, various of the tricks
by means of which the work of prose-construction is habitually
dodged:

5. *Dying metaphors.* A newly invented metaphor assists thought by
evoking a visual image, while on the other hand a metaphor which is
technically "dead" (e.g. *iron resolution*) has in effect reverted to being
an ordinary word and can generally be used without loss of vividness. But in between these two classes there is a huge dump of worn-
out metaphors which have lost all evocative power and are merely
used because they save people the trouble of inventing phrases for
themselves. Examples are: *Ring the changes on, take up the cudgels
for, toe the line, ride roughshod over, stand shoulder to shoulder with,
play into the hands of, no axe to grind, grist to the mill, fishing in
troubled waters, on the order of the day, Achilles' heel, swan song,
hotbed.* Many of these are used without knowledge of their meaning
(what is a "rift," for instance?), and incompatible metaphors are frequently mixed, a sure sign that the writer is not interested in what
he is saying. Some metaphors now current have been twisted out of
their original meaning without those who use them even being aware
of the fact. For example, *toe the line* is sometimes written *tow the line.*
Another example is *the hammer and the anvil,* now always used with
the implication that the anvil gets the worst of it. In real life it is
always the anvil that breaks the hammer, never the other way about:
a writer who stopped to think what he was saying would be aware of
this, and would avoid perverting the original phrase.

6. *Operators* or *verbal false limbs.* These save the trouble of picking
out appropriate verbs and nouns, and at the same time pad each
sentence with extra syllables which give it an appearance of sym-
metry. Characteristic phrases are *render inoperative, militate against,
make contact with, be subjected to, give rise to, give grounds for, have*

the effect of, play a leading part (role) in, make itself felt, take effect, exhibit a tendency to, serve the purpose of, etc., etc. The keynote is the elimination of simple verbs. Instead of being a single word, such as *break, stop, spoil, mend, kill,* a verb becomes a *phrase,* made up of a noun or adjective tacked on to some general-purposes verb such as *prove, serve, form, play, render.* In addition, the passive voice is wherever possible used in preference to the active, and noun constructions are used instead of gerunds *(by examination of* instead of *by examining).* The range of verbs is further cut down by means of the *-ize* and *de-* formations, and the banal statements are given an appearance of profundity by means of the *not un-* formation. Simple conjunctions and prepositions are replaced by such phrases as *with respect to, having regard to, the fact that, by dint of, in view of, in the interests of, on the hypothesis that;* and the ends of sentences are saved by anti-climax by such resounding common-places as *greatly to be desired, cannot be left out of account, a development to be expected in the near future, deserving of serious consideration, brought to a satisfactory conclusion,* and so on and so forth.

7. *Pretentious diction.* Words like *phenomenon, element, individual* (as noun), *objective, categorical, effective, virtual, basic, primary, promote, constitute, exhibit, exploit, utilize, eliminate, liquidate,* are used to dress up simple statement and give an air of scientific impartiality to biased judgments. Adjectives like *epoch-making, epic, historic, unforgettable, triumphant, age-old, inevitable, inexorable, veritable,* are used to dignify the sordid processes of international politics, while writing that aims at glorifying war usually takes on an archaic color, its characteristic words being: *realm, throne, chariot, mailed fist, trident, sword, shield, buckler, banner, jackboot, clarion.* Foreign words and expressions such as *cul de sac, ancien régime, deus ex machina, mutatis mutandis, status quo, gleichschaltung, weltanschauung,* are used to give an air of culture and elegance. Except for the useful abbreviations *i.e., e.g.,* and *etc.,* there is no real need for any of the hundreds of foreign phrases now current in English. Bad writers, and especially scientific, political and sociological writers, are nearly always haunted by the notion that Latin or Greek words are grander than Saxon ones, and unnecessary words like *expedite, ameliorate, predict, extraneous, deracinated, clandestine, subaqueous* and hundreds of others constantly gain ground from their Anglo-Saxon

opposite numbers.[1] The jargon peculiar to Marxist writing (*hyena, hangman, cannibal, petty bourgeois, these gentry, lacquey, flunkey, mad dog, White Guard*, etc.) consists largely of words and phrases translated from Russian, German or French; but the normal way of coining a new word is to use a Latin or Greek root with the appropriate affix and, where necessary, the size formation. It is often easier to make up words of this kind (*deregionalize, impermissible, extramarital, non-fragmentary* and so forth) than to think up the English words that will cover one's meaning. The result, in general, is an increase in slovenliness and vagueness.

8. *Meaningless words.* In certain kinds of writing, particularly in art criticism and literary criticism, it is normal to come across long passages which are almost completely lacking in meaning.[2] Words like *romantic, plastic, values, human, dead, sentimental, natural, vitality,* as used in art criticism, are strictly meaningless, in the sense that they not only do not point to any discoverable object, but are hardly ever expected to do so by the reader. When one critic writes, "The outstanding feature of Mr. X's work is its living quality," while another writes, "The immediately striking thing about Mr. X's work is its peculiar deadness," the reader accepts this as a simple difference of opinion. If words like *black* and *white* were involved, instead of the jargon words *dead* and *living*, he would see at once that language was being used in an improper way. Many political words are similarly abused. The word *Fascism* has now no meaning except in so far as it signifies "something not desirable." The words *democracy, socialism, freedom, patriotic, realistic, justice,* have each of them several different meanings which cannot be reconciled with one another. In the case of a word like *democracy*, not only is there no agreed defini-

---

[1]An interesting illustration of this is the way in which the English flower names which were in use till very recently are being ousted by Greek ones, *snapdragon* becoming *antirrhinum*, *forget-me-not* becoming *myosotis*, etc. It is hard to see any practical reason for this change of fashion: it is probably due to an instinctive turning-away from the more homely word and a vague feeling that the Greek word is scientific.

[2]Example: "Comfort's catholicity of perception and image, strangely Whitman-esque in range, almost the exact opposite in aesthetic compulsion, continues to evoke that trembling atmospheric accumulative hinting at a cruel, an inexorably serene timelessness. . . . Wrey Gardiner scores by aiming at simple bull's-eyes with precision. Only they are not so simple, and through this contented sadness runs more than the surface bitter-sweet of resignation." (*Poetry Quarterly*.)

tion, but the attempt to make one is resisted from all sides. It is almost universally felt that when we call a country democratic we are praising it: consequently the defenders of every kind of régime claim that it is a democracy, and fear that they might have to stop using the word if it were tied down to any one meaning. Words of this kind are often used in a consciously dishonest way. That is, the person who uses them has his own private definition, but allows his hearer to think he means something quite different. Statements like *Marshal Pétain was a true patriot, The Soviet Press is the freest in the world, The Catholic Church is opposed to persecution,* are almost always made with intent to deceive. Other words used in variable meanings, in most cases more or less dishonestly, are: *class, totalitarian, science, progressive, reactionary, bourgeois, equality.*

9. Now that I have made this catalogue of swindles and perversions, let me give another example of the kind of writing that they lead to. This time it must of its nature be an imaginary one. I am going to translate a passage of good English into modern English of the worst sort. Here is a well-known verse from *Ecclesiastes:*

"I returned and saw under the sun, that the race is not to the swift, nor the battle to the strong, neither yet bread to the wise, nor yet riches to men of understanding, nor yet favour to men of skill; but time and chance happeneth to them all."

10. Here it is in modern English:

"Objective considerations of contemporary phenomena compels the conclusion that success or failure in competitive activities exhibits no tendency to be commensurate with innate capacity, but that a considerable element of the unpredictable must invariably be taken into account."

11. This is a parody, but not a very gross one. Exhibit (3), above, for instance, contains several patches of the same kind of English. It will be seen that I have not made a full translation. The beginning and ending of the sentence follow the original meaning fairly closely, but in the middle the concrete illustrations—race, battle, bread—dissolve into the vague phrase "success or failure in competitive activities." This had to be so, because no modern writer of the kind I am discussing—no one capable of using phrases like "objective consideration of contemporary phenomena"—would ever tabulate his thoughts in that precise and detailed way. The whole tendency of modern prose is away from concreteness. Now analyse these two sentences a little more closely. The first contains forty-nine words but only sixty syllables, and all its words are those of everyday life. The second contains thirty-eight words of ninety syllables: eighteen of its words are from Latin roots, and one from Greek. The first sentence contains six vivid images, and only one phrase ("time and chance") that could be called vague. The second contains not a single fresh, arresting phrase, and in spite of its ninety syllables it gives only a shortened version of the meaning contained in the first. Yet without a doubt it is the second kind of sentence that is gaining ground in modern English. I do not want to exaggerate. This kind of writing is not yet universal, and outcrops of simplicity will occur here and there in the worst-written page. Still, if you or I were told to write a few lines on the uncertainty of human fortunes, we should probably come much nearer to my imaginary sentence than to the one from *Ecclesiastes.*

12. As I have tried to show, modern writing at its worst does not consist in picking out words for the sake of their meaning and inventing images in order to make the meaning clearer. It consists in gumming together long strips of words which have already been set in order by someone else, and making the results presentable by sheer humbug. The attraction of this way of writing is that it is easy. It is easier— even quicker, once you have the habit—to say *In my opinion it is not an unjustifiable assumption that* than to say *I think.* If you use ready-made phrases, you not only don't have to hunt about for words; you also don't have to bother with the rhythms of your sentences, since these phrases are generally so arranged as to be more or less euphonious. When you are composing in a hurry—when you are dictating to a stenographer, for instance, or making a public speech— it is natural to fall into a pretentious, Latinized style. Tags like *a consideration which we should do well to bear in mind* or *a conclusion to which all of us would readily assent* will save many a sentence from coming down with a bump. By using stale metaphors, similes and idioms, you save much mental effort, at the cost of leaving your meaning vague, not only for your reader but for yourself. This is the significance of mixed metaphors. The sole aim of a metaphor is to call up a visual image. When these images clash—as in *The Fascist octopus has sung its swan song, the jackboot is thrown into the melting pot*— it can be taken as certain that the writer is not seeing a mental image of the objects he is naming; in other words he is not really thinking. Look again at the examples I gave at the beginning of this essay.

Professor Laski (1) uses five negatives in fifty-three words. One of these is superfluous, making nonsense of the whole passage, and in addition there is the slip *alien* for akin, making further nonsense, and several avoidable pieces of clumsiness which increase the general vagueness. Professor Hogben (2) plays ducks and drakes with a battery which is able to write prescriptions, and, while disapproving of the everyday phrase *put up with*, is unwilling to look *egregious* up in the dictionary and see what it means; (3), if one takes an uncharitable attitude towards it, is simply meaningless: probably one could work out its intended meaning by reading the whole of the article in which it occurs. In (4), the writer knows more or less what he wants to say, but an accumulation of stale phrases chokes him like tea leaves blocking a sink. In (5), words and meaning have almost parted company. People who write in this manner usually have a general emotional meaning—they dislike one thing and want to express solidarity with another—but they are not interested in the detail of what they are saying. A scrupulous writer, in every sentence that he writes, will ask himself at least four questions, thus: What am I trying to say? What words will express it? What image or idiom will make it clearer? Is this image fresh enough to have an effect? And he will probably ask himself two more: Could I put it more shortly? Have I said anything that is avoidably ugly? But you are not obliged to go to all this trouble. You can shirk it by simply throwing your mind open and letting the ready-made phrases come crowding in. They will construct your sentences for you—even think your thoughts for you, to a certain extent—and at need they will perform the important service of partially concealing your meaning even from yourself. It is at this point that the special connection between politics and the debasement of language becomes clear.

13. In our time it is broadly true that political writing is bad writing. Where it is not true, it will generally be found that the writer is some kind of rebel, expressing his private opinions and not a "party line." Orthodoxy, of whatever color, seems to demand a lifeless, imitative style. The political dialects to be found in pamphlets, leading articles, manifestos, White Papers and the speeches of under-secretaries do, of course, vary from party to party, but they are all alike in that one almost never finds in them a fresh, vivid, home-made turn of speech. When one watches some tired hack on the platform mechanically repeating the familiar phrases—*bestial atrocities, iron heel, blood-*

stained tyranny, free peoples of the world, stand shoulder to shoulder
—one often has a curious feeling that one is not watching a live
human being but some kind of dummy: a feeling which suddenly becomes stronger at moments when the light catches the speaker's
spectacles and turns them into blank discs which seem to have no
eyes behind them. And this is not altogether fanciful. A speaker who
uses that kind of phraseology has gone some distance towards turning
himself into a machine. The appropriate noises are coming out of his
larynx, but his brain is not involved as it would be if he were choosing
his words for himself. If the speech he is making is one that he is
accustomed to make over and over again, he may be almost unconscious of what he is saying, as one is when one utters the responses in
church. And this reduced state of consciousness, if not indispensable,
is at any rate favorable to political conformity.

14. In our time, political speech and writing are largely the defence
of the indefensible. Things like the continuance of British rule in
India, the Russian purges and deportations, the dropping of the atom
bombs on Japan, can indeed be defended, but only by arguments
which are too brutal for most people to face, and which do not square
with the professed aims of political parties. Thus political language
has to consist largely of euphemism, question-begging and sheer
cloudy vagueness. Defenceless villages are bombarded from the air,
the inhabitants driven out into the countryside, the cattle machine-
gunned, the huts set on fire with incendiary bullets: this is called
pacification. Millions of peasants are robbed of their farms and sent
trudging along the roads with no more than they can carry: this is
called *transfer of population* or *rectification of frontiers.* People are
imprisoned for years without trial, or shot in the back of the neck or
sent to die of scurvy in Arctic lumber camps: this is called *elimination
of unreliable elements.* Such phraseology is needed if one wants to
name things without calling up mental pictures of them. Consider for
instance some comfortable English professor defending Russian total-
itarianism. He cannot say outright, "I believe in killing off your op-
ponents when you can get good results by doing so." Probably,
therefore, he will say something like this:

"While freely conceding that the Soviet régime exhibits certain
features which the humanitarian may be inclined to deplore, we
must, I think, agree that a certain curtailment of the right to political
opposition is an unavoidable concomitant of transitional periods, and

that the rigors which the Russian people have been called upon to undergo have been amply justified in the sphere of concrete achievement."

15. The inflated style is itself a kind of euphemism. A mass of Latin words falls upon the facts like soft snow, blurring the outlines and covering up all the details. The great enemy of clear language is insincerity. When there is a gap between one's real and one's declared aims, one turns as it were instinctively to long words and exhausted idioms, like a cuttlefish squirting out ink. In our age there is no such thing as "keeping out of politics." All issues are political issues, and politics itself is a mass of lies, evasion, folly, hatred and schizophrenia. When the general atmosphere is bad, language must suffer. I should expect to find—this is a guess which I have not sufficient knowledge to verify—that the German, Russian and Italian languages have all deteriorated in the last ten or fifteen years, as a result of dictatorship.

16. But if thought corrupts language, language can also corrupt thought. A bad usage can spread by tradition and imitation, even among people who should and do know better. The debased language that I have been discussing is in some ways very convenient. Phrases like *a not unjustifiable assumption, leaves much to be desired, would serve no good purpose, a consideration which we should do well to bear in mind,* are a continuous temptation, a packet of aspirins always at one's elbow. Look back through this essay, and for certain you will find that I have again and again committed the very faults I am protesting against. By this morning's post I have received a pamphlet dealing with conditions in Germany. The author tells me that he "felt impelled" to write it. I open it at random, and here is almost the first sentence that I see: ["The Allies] have an opportunity not only of achieving a radical transformation of Germany's social and political structure in such a way as to avoid a nationalistic reaction in Germany itself, but at the same time of laying the foundations of a co-operative and unified Europe." You see, he "feels impelled" to write —feels, presumably, that he has something new to say—and yet his words, like cavalry horses answering the bugle, group themselves automatically into the familiar dreary pattern. This invasion of one's mind by ready-made phrases *(lay the foundations, achieve a radical transformation)* can only be prevented if one is constantly on guard against them, and every such phrase anaesthetizes a portion of one's brain.

17. I said earlier that the decadence of our language is probably curable. Those who deny this would argue, if they produced an argument at all, that language merely reflects existing social conditions, and that we cannot influence its development by any direct tinkering with words and constructions. So far as the general tone or spirit of a language goes, this may be true, but it is not true in detail. Silly words and expressions have often disappeared, not through any evolutionary process but owing to the conscious action of a minority. Two recent examples were *explore every avenue* and *leave no stone unturned*, which were killed by the jeers of a few journalists. There is a long list of flyblown metaphors which could similarly be got rid of if enough people would interest themselves in the job; and it should also be possible to laugh the *not un-* formation out of existence,[1] to reduce the amount of Latin and Greek in the average sentence, to drive out foreign phrases and strayed scientific words, and, in general, to make pretentiousness unfashionable. But all these are minor points. The defence of the English language implies more than this, and perhaps it is best to start by saying what it does *not* imply.
18. To begin with it has nothing to do with archaism, with the salvaging of obsolete words and turns of speech, or with the setting up of a "standard English" which must never be departed from. On the contrary, it is especially concerned with the scrapping of every word or idiom which has outworn its usefulness. It has nothing to do with correct grammar and syntax, which are of no importance so long as one makes one's meaning clear, or with the avoidance of Americanisms, or with having what is called a "good prose style." On the other hand it is not concerned with fake simplicity and the attempt to make written English colloquial. Nor does it even imply in every case preferring the Saxon word to the Latin one, though it does imply using the fewest and shortest words that will cover one's meaning. What is above all needed is to let the meaning choose the word, and not the other way about. In prose, the worst thing one can do with words is to surrender to them. When you think of a concrete object, you think wordlessly, and then, if you want to describe the thing you have been visualizing you probably hunt about till you find the exact words that seem to fit it. When you think of something abstract you are more inclined to use words from the start, and unless you make a conscious

---

[1]One can cure oneself of the *not un-* formation by memorizing this sentence: *A not unblack dog was chasing a not unsmall rabbit across a not ungreen field.*

effort to prevent it, the existing dialect will come rushing in and do the job for you, at the expense of blurring or even changing your meaning. Probably it is better to put off using words as long as possible and get one's meaning as clear as one can through pictures or sensations. Afterwards one can choose—not simply *accept*—the phrases that will best cover the meaning, and then switch round and decide what impression one's words are likely to make on another person. This last effort of the mind cuts out all stale or mixed images, all prefabricated phrases, needless repetitions, and humbug and vagueness generally. But one can often be in doubt about the effect of a word or a phrase, and one needs rules that one can rely on when instinct fails. I think the following rules will cover most cases:

(i) Never use a metaphor, simile or other figure of speech which you are used to seeing in print.

(ii) Never use a long word where a short one will do.

(iii) If it is possible to cut a word out, always cut it out.

(iv) Never use the passive where you can use the active.

(v) Never use a foreign phrase, a scientific word or a jargon word if you can think of an everyday English equivalent.

(vi) Break any of these rules sooner than say anything outright barbarous.

These rules sound elementary, and so they are, but they demand a deep change of attitude in anyone who has grown used to writing in the style now fashionable. One could keep all of them and still write bad English, but one could not write the kind of stuff that I quoted in those five specimens at the beginning of this article.

19. I have not here been considering the literary use of language, but merely language as an instrument for expressing and not for concealing or preventing thought. Stuart Chase and others have come near to claiming that all abstract words are meaningless, and have used this as a pretext for advocating a kind of political quietism. Since you don't know what Fascism is, how can you struggle against Fascism? One need not swallow such absurdities as this, but one ought to recognize that the present political chaos is connected with the decay of language, and that one can probably bring about some improvement by starting at the verbal end. If you simplify your English, you are freed from the worst follies of orthodoxy. You cannot speak any of the necessary dialects, and when you make a stupid remark its

stupidity will be obvious, even to yourself. Political language—and
with variations this is true of all political parties, from Conservatives
to Anarchists—is designed to make lies sound truthful and murder
respectable, and to give an appearance of solidity to pure wind.
One cannot change this all in a moment, but one can at least change
one's own habits, and from time to time one can even, if one jeers
loudly enough, send some worn-out and useless phrase—some *jackboot, Achilles' heel, hotbed, melting pot, acid test, veritable inferno*
or other lump of verbal refuse—into the dustbin where it belongs.

> Orwell, in 1946, called attention to the impact of international
> politics on the language of public discussion. . . . [his] point was
> that the modern world calls for more than mythology and incan-
> tation. Modern technology has given us new power, new politics,
> and new ways to communicate their impact. To deal with this, to
> learn to accept it, we need an entire new political vocabulary—a
> Newspeak. Nor is this an unfulfilled need. . . . Redefinition . . .
> shades into . . . the complete inversion of normal meaning:
>
>> Policy-makers . . . fear headlines about "highest losses of
>> the war" will fuel the arguments of U. S. doves. . . . "It's
>> hard to explain to people," conceded a high officer, "that the
>> higher casualties mean we're doing a better job." (*Wall
>> Street Journal,* "Washington Wire," March 10, 1967)
>
> . . . Another important Newspeak technique is to depersonalize
> the other side:
>
>> "I got me a VC, man. I got at least two of them bastards."
>
> . . . "A VC," the object of "search and destroy missions," the
> results of which are given daily in "body count" figures. The
> dispatch goes on:
>
>> The Marines ordered a . . . corporal to go down . . . to pull
>> out their victims . . . three children riddled with bullets. . . .
>> (UPI dispatch, Aug. 3, 1965, from Chan Sun)
>
> He got himself some children. . . . one might say that political
> language appears designed to eliminate the appearance of a cred-
> ibility gap and to reduce the onus of social disapproval falling
> on the unavoidably severe methods required to root out enemy
> sympathizers.
>
> Edward and Onora Nell,
>
> "War Words," *College English*

What I have most wanted to do through out the past ten years is to make political writing into an art. My starting point is always a feeling of partisanship, a sense of injustice.

... I write ... because there is some lie that I want to expose, some fact to which I want to draw attention, and my initial concern is to get a hearing.

... The job is to reconcile my ingrained likes and dislikes with the essentially public, non-individual activities that this age forces on all of us.

What I have doubleplus wanted through ten anteyears is to make politwrite good form. My startfeel is always crimethink.

... I write because there is some untrue I want to openput, some true I want circumlooked, and my startfeel is intercom.

... The job is to rekcile my intrabuilded goodfeels and ungoodfeels with the mostwise unselful acts the nowtime onputs everybody.

Joseph Foley and James Ayer,

"Orwell in English and Newspeak:
A Computer Translation,"
College Composition and Communication

Pacification. Killing all the other side in a given area.
Defoliation. Killing all the hostile vegetation in a given area.
Peace offensive. 1. A flurry of diplomatic activity aimed at persuading the other side to engage in unconditional discussion (q.v.). 2. Communist propaganda masking an intention to continue aggression.
Unconditional discussions. Truce negotiations occurring without a prior demand by the other side that we stop bombing North Vietnam.

Richard L. Lingeman,

"Glossary of a Revolution,"
San Francisco Sunday Examiner and Chronicle,
May 27th, 1967

In "Our National Mania for Correctness," Donald J. Lloyd echoes the argument of George Orwell that emphasis in language use should be placed, not on correctness, but on clarity. He contends that academic obfuscation results from an obsession with conformity. He also says that spoken American English is wittier and clearer than written American English—a belief supported by the Cratis Williams article on Mountain Speech. Mr. Lloyd maintains that some of this wit could be preserved in print by concentrating on thought, not style. Is there any evidence for his theory?

Our National Mania for Correctness

Donald J. Lloyd

Every now and then the editors of the university presses let out a disgruntled bleat about the miserable writing done by scholars, even those who are expert in literary fields; and from time to time there are letters and editorials in our national reviews bewailing some current academic malpractice with the English language. At present, even *PMLA* (the Publications of the Modern Language Association), traditionally the repository of some of the worst writing done by researchers, is trying to herd its authors toward more lucid exposition.

From *The American Scholar*, Vol. XXI, No. iii (Summer, 1952), by permission of Donald J. Lloyd.

And at two recent meetings of the august Mediaeval Academy, one at Boston and one at Dumbarton Oaks, bitter remarks were passed about the failure of specialists in the Middle Ages to present their findings in some form palatable to the general reader, so that he can at least understand what they are writing about.

2. Even admitting that a really compelling style is the result of years of cultivation, much scholarly writing is certainly worse than it needs to be. But it is not alone in this. Generally speaking, the writing of literate Americans whose primary business is not writing but something else is pretty bad. It is muddy, backward, convoluted and self-strangled; it is only too obviously the product of a task approached unwillingly and accomplished without satisfaction or zeal. Except for the professionals among us, we Americans are hell on the English language. I am not in touch with the general run of British writing by non-professionals, but I suspect that it is nothing to make those islanders smug, either.

3. Furthermore, almost any college professor, turning the spotlight with some relief from himself and his colleagues to his students, will agree that their writing stinks to high heaven, too. It is a rare student who can write what he has to write with simplicity, lucidity and euphony, those qualities singled out by Somerset Maugham; far more graduating seniors are candidates for a remedial clinic than can pass a writing test with honors. And freshman writing is forever the nightmare of the teachers of composition, as it would be of their colleagues if the latter could not escape to the simple inanities of their objective tests.

4. Yet it was not always so. I have on my desk a little manuscript from the fourteenth century written by an unknown author, which I am in the process of editing. When I read it to one of my classes, as I occasionally do, with no more modernization than my own Great Lakes pronunciation and the substitution of a word for one which has become obsolete, it is a simple, clear and engaging document. "Where is any man nowadays that asketh how I shall love God and my fellow-Christians?" it begins. "How I shall flee sin and serve God truly as a true Christian man should? What man is there that will learn the true law of God, which he biddeth every Christian man to keep upon pain of damnation in hell without end? . . . Unnethe [scarcely] is there any lewd man or lewd woman that can rightly well say his Pater Noster, his Ave Maria, and his Creed, and sound

the words out readily as they should. But when they play Christmas games about the fire, therein will they not fail. Those must be said out without stumbling for dread of smiting. But if a lewd man should be smited now for each failing that he maketh in saying of his Pater Noster, his Ave Maria, and his Creed, I trowe he should be smited at the full." And so on, to the beautiful poetic line, "Then think it not heavy to dwell with thy mother in her wide house, thou that laist in the strait chamber of her womb." The spelling in the original is hectic, and the capitalization and punctuation sporadic, to say the least.

5. Yet there was a man who knew what he had to say and set out about saying it, with no nonsense and no fumbling. He aimed for his audience and, judging by the dog-ears and sweat-marks on the book, which is about the size of one of our pocket books, he hit it. Why cannot we do as well in our time? Indeed, the eighteenth century was about the last age in which almost any man, if he was literate at all, could set down his thoughts—such as they were—so that they did not have to be excavated by the reader. We have an abundance of letters, diaries, pamphlets, and other papers from that period, and they are well written. It was the age, we may recall, not only of Boswell and Johnson, but of Pepys and Franklin as well, and of a host of other men whose main legacy to us was a simple, direct, work-manlike style, sufficient to the man and to the occasion, which said what it had to say and said it well. With the end of that century we go into the foggy, foggy darkness, and God knows whether we shall ever find our way out of it—as a people, that is, as a nation of thinking men and women with something to say.

6. Nevertheless, there is no question what makes our writing bad, or what we shall have to do to better it. We shall simply have to isolate and root out a monomania which now possesses us, which impedes all language study and inhibits all mastery of our native tongue—all mastery, that is, on paper; for as speakers of English, we Americans are loving and effective cultivators of our expression. I recall the gas station attendant who was filling my car. The gasoline foamed to the top of the tank, and he shut off the pump. "Whew!" I said, "that nearly went over." "When you see whitecaps," he replied, "you better stop." "You better had," I said, lost in admiration. But if you had given him a pencil, he would have chewed the end off before he got one word on paper.

7. The demon which possesses us is our mania for correctness. It dominates our minds from the first grade to the graduate school; it is the first and often the only thing we think of when we think of our language. Our spelling must be "correct"—even if the words are ill-chosen; our "usage" must be "correct"—even though any possible substitute expression, however crude, would be perfectly clear; our punctuation must be "correct"—even though practices surge and change with the passing of years, and differ from book to book, periodical to periodical. Correct! That's what we've got to be, and the idea that we've got to be correct rests like a soggy blanket on our brains and our hands whenever we try to write.

8. This mania for correctness is another legacy from the eighteenth century, but it did not get a real grip on us until well into the nineteenth. Its power over us today is appalling. Among my other tasks, I teach advanced courses in the English language to students preparing to teach. Most of these are seniors and graduate students, and in the summer especially, there is a sprinkling of older men and women, experienced teachers, who are sweating out a master's degree. They have had courses in "English" throughout their schooling. But of the nature and structure of the English language, the nature of language habits, the relation of speech to writing, and the differences in usage which arise from dialect and from differing occupational and educational demands—of all these, they know nothing at all. Nor do they come to me expecting to learn about these. They want to know two things: what correct usage is and how you beat it into the kids' heads. That there are other considerations important to an English teacher is news to many of them. What they get from me is a good long look at their language.

9. To trace this monolithic concentration on usage is to pursue a vicious circle, with the linguists on the outside. The literate public seems to get it from the English teachers, and the teachers get it from the public. The attitudes and pronouncements on language of a Jacques Barzun, a Wilson Follett, a Bernard De Voto, or a Norman Lewis ("How Correct Must Correct English Be?") mean more to English teachers than anything said by the most distinguished professional students of language—such as Leonard Bloomfield, Robert Hall or Charles Carpenter Fries. Correct usage is pursued and discussed, furthermore, without much reference to the actual writing of literary men. Now and again I amuse myself by blue-penciling a

current magazine such as the *Saturday Review* or *Collier's* against
the rules. I have to report that error is rampant, if variation is to
be considered error. The boys just don't seem to pay attention to
the rules. Moreover, having seen some of their first drafts, I am
pretty sure that what conformity they do display is the work of their
wives, secretaries, editors, proofreaders and typesetters, rather than
their own. It takes a determined effort to beat the old Adam out of a
readable manuscript.

10. Thus it is only the determined, consciously creative professional
who can build his work on the actual language of men. In a recent
issue of the *Saturday Review,* I stumbled on a quotation from Wolf-
gang Langewiesche. "Well, it isn't crowned by no castle, that's for
sure," he wrote, "and by no cathedral either." My eyes popped, and
I read it again. I liked it. It looked right; it sounded right; it had a
fine Chaucerian swing to it. But I bet it cost him some blood and a
fifth of Scotch to get it into print. In my own limited publication,
I find "a historical" changed to "an historical," all my "further's"
changed to "farther" and all my "farther's" to "further," "than us"
watered down to "than we," and many, many more. How E. M.
Forster got by with "the author he thinks," and got it reprinted in a
freshman handbook a few pages along from the prohibition of such
locutions baffles me. A phony standardization of usage appears in
print, the work of editors unconscious of the ultimate meaning of
what they do.

11. The result of all this is that a wet hand of fear rests on the heart of
every nonprofessional writer who merely has a lot of important knowledge to communicate. He writes every sentence with a self-conscious
horror of doing something wrong. It is always a comfort to him if
he can fit himself into some system, such as that of a business or
governmental office which provides him with a model. It is thus that
gobbledegook comes into being. I once braced a distinguished soci-
ologist, a student of occupational myths and attitudes, about the
convoluted, mainly nominal turgidity of his writing. He apparently
admitted verbs into his sentences the way we admit DP's into the
United States, reluctantly and with pain. In speech he was racy, confident and compelling, a brilliant lecturer. "It's the only way I can get
my work into the periodicals," he told me blandly. "If it's clear and
simple, they don't think it's scholarly." With what relief the peda-
gogues subside into pedagese!

12. If we really want to get good writing from people who know things, so that we can come to learn what they know as easily as we learn from their talk, we can do it in a generation or so. In school and out, in print and out, we can leave usage to its natural nurse, the unforced imitation of the practices which are actually current among educated people. We can use our English courses in school and college, not to give drill on questionable choices among common alternatives, demanding that one be taken as right and the others as wrong, but to give practice in reading and writing. We can learn to read and write for the idea, and go for the idea without regard for anything else. Then our young people will come to maturity confidently using their pencils to find out what they think and get it down on paper; then our scholars will come to write simply, clearly and brilliantly what they brilliantly know.

13. In our speech we have arrived, I think, at a decency of discourse which is conducive to effective expression. We listen, with a grave courteous attention, to massive patterns of speaking different from our own because they come from differences in dialect and social status; we listen without carping and without a mean contempt. Furthermore, we participate; we go with a speaker through halts and starts, over abysses of construction, filling in the lacunae without hesitation; we discount inadvertencies and disregard wrong words, and we arrive in genial good will with the speaker at his meaning. In this atmosphere, our speech has thrived, and the ordinary American is in conversation a confident, competent expressive being. In writing he is something else again.

14. No one flourishes in an atmosphere of repression. It is possible, of course, for a person with special aptitudes and a special drive to bull his way past the prohibitions and achieve an individual style. But with the negative attitude that attends all our writing, those whose main interest lies elsewhere are inhibited by fear of "error" and the nagging it stirs up from setting pen to paper, until the sight of a blank white page gives them the shakes. It is no wonder that their expression is halting and ineffective. They cannot fulfill the demands of a prissy propriety and trace the form of an idea at the same time. They thus arrive at adulthood victims of the steely eye of Mr. Sherwin Cody, whose bearded face stares at them from the countless ads for his correspondence school, demanding, "Do YOU make these mistakes in English?" The locutions he lists are not mistakes, and Mr. Cody knows they are not; but his readers do not know it, and they do not know that they don't matter anyway.

15. For usage doesn't matter. What matters is that we get done what we have to do, and get said what we have to say. Sufficient conformity is imposed upon us by the patterns of our language and by the general practices of its users so that we do not have to run the idea of conformity into the ground by carping about trivial erratics in expression. Why in this matter of language alone complete conformity should be considered a virtue—except to typists, printers and typesetters—it is difficult to see (unless, perhaps, we are using it as a covert and pusillanimous means of establishing our own superiority). In our other concerns in life, we prize individuality; why in this one matter we should depart from a principle that otherwise serves us well is a puzzle for fools and wise men to ponder, especially since there is no general agreement on what to conform to, and one man's correctness is another's error. Not until we come to our senses— teachers, editors, writers and readers together—and stop riding each other's backs, will the casual, colorful, amused, ironic and entertaining talk of Americans find its way into print. We should all be happy to see it there.

> Nevertheless, the difference in social acceptability between *I ain't* and I am not, between *hern* and *hers,* and so forth, is a real fact. If my child is likely to run into trouble later on for saying *I done it* or *hisn,* I will try to keep him from getting into the habit of using those forms which are actually not acceptable socially and which may cause others to react unfavorably towards him. But, if I am sensible about it, I will realize that the reason I want him to avoid these "incorrect" forms is not any inherent badness or evil character that they may have, but a purely practical consideration, that of their social acceptability. His choice of language will be used by others as a purely arbitrary means of classifying him socially among the sheep or the goats. All we need to do in the case of *I ain't,* etc., is to re-word the traditional instructions, and say that we avoid using such turns of speech, not because they are "bad" or "wrong" or ungrammatical," but because they are socially unacceptable. Of course, as soon as people in any given group stop treating, say, *he don't* as socially unacceptable, it automatically becomes "correct."
>
> Robert A. Hall, Jr.,
>
> *Linguistics and Your Language*